Personal
Skill Building for
the Emerging Manager

Printed in the United States

Printing (*last digit*): 9 8 7 6 5 4 3 2 1

Library of Congress Cataloging in Publication Data

Pinkstaff, Marlene Arthur, 1936–
    Personal skill building for the emerging manager.

    Bibliography: p. 191
    1. Supervision of employees.   2. Executive
ability. I.   Pinkstaff, Dick, 1933– joint author.
II.   Title.
HF5549.P4718   658.3'02   79–16920
ISBN 0–8436–0785–8

Contents

Introduction

Personal Skill Building for the Emerging Manager contains thirteen chapters, each supplemented with skill-building suggestions and pointers. The text of each chapter is followed by an application section, which consists of exercises, an idea for improvement, and a review section. The suggested answers to the review questions follow chapter thirteen.

For best results, read and complete one chapter at a time. You may wish to complete one chapter a day or one a week at your own pace, but do not allow more than a week to elapse between chapters.

Application Sections are designed for each participant to complete individually. However, you are encouraged to involve your superior in these exercises. In lieu of a supportive superior, you may use a peer or a good friend. The more meaningful your practice, the more successful you will be in acquiring skills.

Foreword:

What is in this Book for You

The new supervisor, department head, staff assistant, sales or marketing manager, or secretary's success will depend on the management skills and techniques that he or she possesses and implements.

These personal development skills studies have met the test of practical application by supervisors and managers of hundreds of diversified companies. In response to the extensive demand for basic personal and development skills for management and potential managers, these skills studies have been developed and prepared in this convenient self-teaching workbook format.

Personal development and management skills are a basic requirement for proficiency in supervision at any level. These skills can be acquired by any person in business at any level of management who will study to understand them and conscientiously practice to perfect them.

This know-how manual for supervisory self-development should not be allowed to lie on the shelf. It should be kept close at hand for reference and consultation by everyone in any management or premanagement position.

The new and also the potential supervisor will enjoy this book and find it helpful in acquiring skills necessary to be effective participants in management. The experienced manager will also appreciate the value of this book in the enlargement and upgrading of management skills.

More supervisors fail from lack of skill in practical supervision than from lack of real knowledge about supervision. This book goes beyond the 'what to do' and prescribes practical suggestions, pointers, and work guides for improvement of essential leadership and supervisory skills.

CHAPTER 1

The Supervisor's Role

You have been made a supervisor, or are considering the management profession, because you have distinguished yourself and have qualities that set you apart from other employees. You have demonstrated that you have skill capabilities. Now, as a supervisor, you are called on to demonstrate your capabilities to lead others. When you are able to persuade others to follow you, to follow your example, then you become a leader.

Before becoming a supervisor, your responsibilities were restricted to handling your own job. Now, your responsibilities also include supervising the performance of other employees.

Prior to becoming a supervisor, it was much easier to maintain good working human relations. If you kept your lines clear with your immediate supervisor, you probably did not have any other assigned human relations responsibilities. Now, however, you are responsible for maintaining good relations with both your superior and your employees (or subordinates).

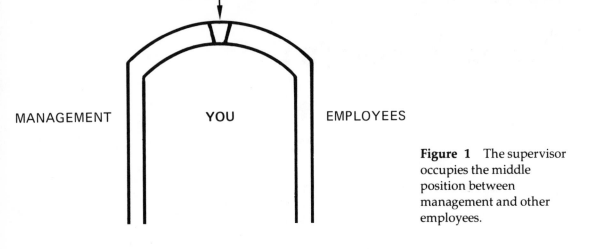

Figure 1 The supervisor occupies the middle position between management and other employees.

THE SUPERVISOR'S POSITION

It has been accurately described that the position of a supervisor is truly one of being in the middle.

Figure 1 shows that the supervisor is the keystone in the arch, the central piece that holds the structure together between the needs of management and employees. The effective supervisor must balance and coordinate the needs of the company with the needs of people.

DEMANDS AND FORCES
ON A COMPANY

To give you a better understanding of the needs of your company, this section builds a step-by-step needs structure that shows five demands and forces on a company.

Why does your company exist? Like most companies, it is in business to make a profit by performing and/or providing a service/product. Figure 2 represents the company with its reason for existence — *to make a reasonable and fair profit.* To satisfy the profit need, a company must perform or provide a service or product. This service or product is provided to meet the needs of the customer. The customer's demands (on a company profit need), as shown in Figure 3, will be examined first.

Figure 2 A company is in business to make a profit.

Whether or not a customer buys from a company depends on the company's ability to produce the product or service and to satisfy the demands of the customer. Some customer demands include supplying a service and/or product with the:

> desired quality
> desired quantity
> desired cost
> at desired time

These four customer demands directly affect the profit need of the company.

A second demand on a company and its profit need comes from the *Owners,* as shown in Figure 4. This demand is usually in the form of earnings per share dividends. Owners demand a reasonable return on their investment.

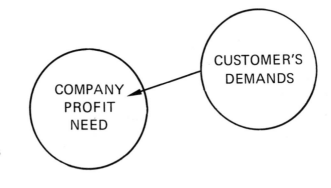

Figure 3 Customers' demands on a company's profit need.

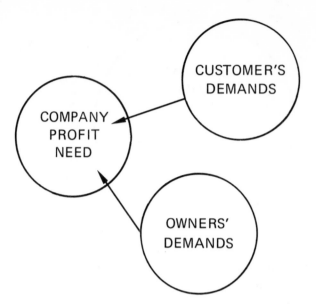

Figure 4 Owners' demands on a company's profit need.

A third demand on a company comes from the *Community*. Demands that the community might make on the company include:

being a good contributor

being a good neighbor and taxpayer

dealing with pollution and environmental conditions

purchasing supplies and parts locally

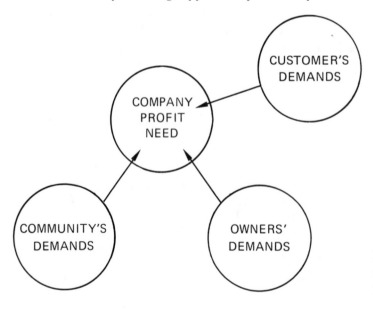

Figure 5 Community's demands on a company's profit need.

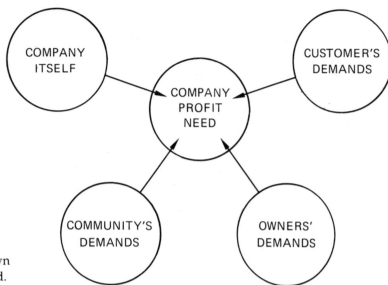

Figure 6 Company's own demands on its profit need.

A fourth demand on a company and its need to make a profit comes from within the *Company* itself. Examples of this demand might include:

money for research and growth

money for education and seminars

new space or new building

any expansion program

The fifth demand on a company is made by the *Employees*. The employees make demands on the company before they will agree to work in it or to continue their employment. Employees require:

adequate wages

stable employment

good working conditions

employee benefit program

good supervision

These demands now surround the company; all exert pressure on the profit need of the company.

Let us review the importance of these demands on the company. We can make four observations of what these demands mean to *you* as a supervisor:

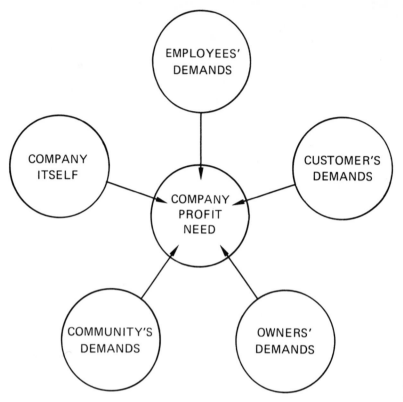

Figure 7 Employees' demands on a company's profit need.

1. The needs are conflicting.
2. The needs are difficult to meet.
3. Your role is to try to bring the profit needs of the company and the employee needs together.
4. These needs provide real challenge in maintaining a team spirit.

THE SUPERVISOR'S JOB

The supervisor's job really involves a double allegiance—to the company (your management) you represent your workers; and to the employees you represent the company. This double allegiance may cause you some trouble from time to time. Management may see you as siding with your employees, whereas the workers may feel you are on the side of the management/company.

As shown earlier in Figure 1, the supervisor's position is the keystone in an arch; thus, you are the *key* between management and the workers. You belong to and must identify with *both* management and workers. Although you have an allegiance to both of these groups, you should never play one against the other. Instead, you should try to make the goals (needs) of the company also the goals (needs) of the employees. In performing this difficult task, you should not divide your allegiance between company and employees. Since you are in management, you represent the interest of your employees to the company; and because you are close to the work force, you can communicate your company's goals to the workers. To be successful, a supervisor must maintain close contact with the work force without sacrificing usefulness as a member of the management team. As a member of management, you represent the company and its policies both to the employees you supervise and to others with whom you and your workers have contact.

All too often, a supervisor will begin to explain a policy to her employees by stating: "I know this is a silly rule and I don't agree with it, but this is what *they* say we are to do. . . ."

What is wrong with this approach? The supervisor is not fulfilling the dual responsibility to the company and the employees because she is trying to be identified as one of the workers again. A supervisor should explain why *we* do or are doing it this way instead of saying that *they* told us or said we must do.

One of the most difficult problems for a supervisor to overcome concerns production. Regardless of what function you supervise, your job is to get work done through people.

As a supervisor, you are an overhead expense to a company because you produce nothing in the way of a product. For you to be a successful supervisor, you must meet production needs, whatever the product or service, by blending the needs and demands of your work force and of your company.

As a supervisor, you have been given the responsibility of getting work done through people. This responsibility can often be seen in meeting schedules and in producing a product/service in terms of quality, quantity, and cost.

To fulfill this responsibility of producing within the guidelines of quality, quantity, and cost, a supervisor is given the following management tools:

The Essentials of Production

MATERIALS   MONEY   MACHINERY   METHODS   PEOPLE

Although a supervisor is concerned with all of these tools, the one of most concern usually is people. Management has most often been defined as getting work done through *people*. This definition can be enlarged to include the word *enable:* The manager's role is to *enable* workers to do their job.

What goal should you have in working through people? To be successful in management, you must blend the basic need of the company (to make a profit by performing or providing a service/product) by working through the needs of your people. A supervisor must attempt to make the profit need or goal of the company the goal and objective of each individual employee. Successful supervisors can use many methods to reach this objective.

The real questions to be answered in managing become:

1. How can you get the most of your people?
2. How can you demonstrate that the employee needs/demands are fulfilled when the company's profit need is satisfied?
3. How can you motivate the employees to contribute to the overall effectiveness and profitability of your company?

SUMMARY

Being the person in the middle is not a bad situation. Using your skills to get the best of materials, money, machinery, methods, and people is both challenging and rewarding. Your job as supervisor is to serve as the supporting link between management and your team members. You must work at blending the *they* and the *we* into an *us*. The company that learns to work as a team will be the company that develops and gets the full potential of the tools of management.

Understanding the demands made on your company better enables you to meet the needs that confront you as a supervisor. Developing the management skills that enable you to meet the needs of your team is one of your primary tasks as a supervisor.

The following chapters will explore and practice application techniques that will help you meet the needs of both the employees and the company.

THE SUPERVISOR'S ROLE:
SKILL-BUILDING APPLICATION
THE TOOLS OF MANAGEMENT

Give at least one example of how you as a supervisor can increase profits of your company and can advance your own career through the management tools you have.

Material: _____

_____

_____

_____

_____

Money: _____

_____

_____

_____

Machinery: _____

_____

_____

_____

Methods: _____

_____

_____

_____

_____

People: _____

_____

_____

_____

_____

COMPANY KNOWLEDGE DEMANDS

Your company has the same needs as discussed and pictured in chapter 1. Answer the following questions: your answers will comprise a base of information that you will need to answer your employees' questions.

What are the profits of your company? _____

_____

_____

_____

Name the major customers of your company. _____

_____

_____

_____

List the major owners of your company. _____

_____

_____

_____

What are some of the demands made on your company by the community? _____

_____

_____

_____

What demands is your company making on itself? (expansion, research, buildings?) _____

_____

_____

_____

WE versus THEY

Probably one of the most common faults in any organization is a problem in dual responsibility of a supervisor. This problem is seen in organizations as a *we–they* situation. Workers and supervisors often refer to management as an impersonal *they*. Supervisors should strive to understand the *we* benefits versus *they* benefits.

List three examples of when you have used the *we* approach; also list your results.

Example of *we*   Results

1. _____   _____

   _____   _____

   _____   _____

   _____   _____

   _____   _____

   _____   _____

2. _____   _____

   _____   _____

   _____   _____

   _____   _____

   _____   _____

3. _____   _____

   _____   _____

   _____   _____

   _____   _____

   _____   _____

IDEAS FOR IMPROVEMENT

From what you have learned in this chapter, list one or more specific actions that you intend to initiate within the next thirty days.

1. _____

_____

_____

_____

_____

_____

_____

2. _____

_____

_____

_____

_____

_____

_____

3. _____

_____

_____

_____

_____

_____

REVIEW QUESTIONS

T   F   1.   The supervisor is the middle person between management and employees.

               2.   A company is in existence to make a _____.

               3.   In order to make a profit, the company must offer a

_____

or _____

               4.   Name the five sources of demand that put pressure on the profit need of a company.

_____

_____

_____

_____

_____

T   F   5.   An employee has the right to choose his supervisor.

               6.   Employee turnover, poor instruction, grievances not listened to, and poor attitudes are the result of poor

_____

               7.   A supervisor has a dual responsibility to _____

_____and _____

               8.   Name the five management tools of production.

_____   _____

_____   _____

_____

T   F   9.   The most important of the five tools is money.

             10.   Management is most often defined as getting work done through _____.

CHAPTER 2

Skill in Analyzing Your Time

"**W**here does the time go? I never seem to have time to do my job," say supervisors throughout the country. They admit that one of their toughest management problems is self-management—how to make result-getting use of personal time.

COMMON PROBLEM

"I'm always putting out fires! I never have time to do anything but chase fires, and half the time they're false alarms."

"At the end of the day, I feel like a bird caught in a badminton game."

If you sometimes have these feelings about what happens to your day, don't despair. You are not alone. Supervisors say that one of their greatest problems is finding the time to handle the functions and details for which they are responsible. The many activities that require a technical supervisor's time are listed in Table 1.

TABLE 1.

ACTIVITES OF A TECHNICAL SUPERVISOR

Activity	Percentage of Time
Quality	_____
Work progress	_____
Personnel administration	_____
Personal relations and other nonjob-related topics	_____
Equipment and fixtures	_____
Supervisor performance of an operation	_____
Materials	_____
Employee job performance	_____
Production schedule	_____
Grievances	_____
Injury, illness	_____
Housekeeping	_____
Work standards	_____
Safety	_____
Meetings	_____
Miscellaneous and unknown	_____
	100%

The activities listed in Table 2 are typical of the use of an office supervisor's time.

Before continuing with this chapter, refer to the more appropriate‎ breakdown for your present job (technical, Table 1, or office supervisor, Table 2). Opposite each activity record what you feel is a representative percent of time that you presently spend on each study.

TABLE 2.
ACTIVITIES OF AN OFFICE SUPERVISOR

Activity	Your Estimated Percentage of Time
Work performance standards	_____
Handling incoming and outgoing reports	_____
Paperwork flow	_____
Telephone	_____
Checking on work progress	_____
Assigning work	_____
Interviewing (new employees, transfers, problem employees)	_____
Memo writing	_____
Reading and checking incoming mail	_____
Analyzing source data	_____
Improving systems and procedures	_____
Meetings	_____
Office equipment maintenance	_____
Requisitioning supplies	_____
Personal	_____
Miscellaneous	_____
	100%

INVEST TIME TO SAVE TIME

People who are successful in managing their time tell us that some basic skills are involved. These skills can be learned. Through exercise, drill, and practice, it is possible to have the time you need. Invest some time in your own self-development to save time on the job.

HOW TO ANALYZE THE USE OF TIME

Supervisor Pat Leach never knows where her time goes. She starts her rounds to check her office. On the way, she learns of a calculator that needs repair. So back to her phone for a call to the shop; but the phone rings as she gets there—it is her supervisor. "No, Boss, I do not have those figures yet, but I'll give you a call." Just then, a worker sticks her head in the office to say she is out of key-punch cards. ("I should have taken care of that last night," Pat thinks to herself, "but I just do not have time for everything.") . . . and so on through the day.

"When the disposal of time is surrendered to the chance of incidents, chaos will reign," Victor Hugo wrote.

Activity Study

Begin to master the clock by making a study of exactly what you do with your time. Keep a log of your activities for a week or two. This study may highlight many time-saving steps you can take. Review the log with such questions as these in mind.

What activities have recurred regularly?

Was proper attention given to each of your major functions?

How often were less important matters handled first?

Where could time have been saved by combining problems and making one contact?

Could time have been saved with a phone call or a brief note?

How often were problems picked up and shuffled without decisive action?

HOW TO GET THE TIME TO PLAN

Many harried supervisors may feel that they do not even have time to make time-saving plans. But without time planning, confusion, wasted effort, and activity duplication will result.

Planning Suggestion

The successful supervisor follows these basic rules in controlling his time. **Find time to plan.** No matter how busy the day or pressing the events, arrange your schedule so that you have some uninterrupted time during each day and each week. It may only be ten minutes at the beginning and end of each day, but *make* the time and *take* the time for an unhurried, uninterrupted review of accomplishments and coming tasks.

HOW TO PLAN YOUR TIME

Clearly, some method is needed to begin to organize time. The simpler the system, the better. If the system is too detailed and inflexible, you may find yourself spending too much time revising the schedule.

Practical Pointers

To develop skill in planning your time:

Get into the habit of using a calendar reminder to plan your days and weeks.

Each day, jot down a list of the things you expect to accomplish on the following day. As action is taken, cross each item off the list. A planning sheet is a simple but effective way to budget time and at the same time not to overlook details.

HOW TO SET PRIORITIES

Unless you are on guard, it is only natural to do first the things that you like to do or find easy to do and to put off until tomorrow the more difficult or disagreeable chores.

To make the most productive use of your time, try to set up some priorities for the items in your daily plan. This may simply mean listing the things you plan to do in the order of their importance.

Priority Procedures

Practice setting priorities each day as you list the things to be accomplished. Assign to each item one of three general weightings:

1. MUST be done: Steps absolutely essential to the day's work or to the success of future plans. Prompt action needed.
2. SHOULD be done: Activities that require attention some time during the day, but that are less urgent than *must* items.
3. CAN be done: Less essential details that should be handled as time permits. If an emergency arises, these activities are more postponable than are *must* or *should* items.

It may help to visualize these three priority levels as three rings of a

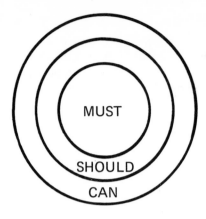

Figure 8 Daily time target of priority levels.

bull's eye. Priorities help to round out your daily time target. With repeated drill, you will find that setting priorities becomes automatic. When new problems come up unexpectedly, compare their importance with the priority of the other tasks competing for your time.

HOW TO DELEGATE

Skill in delegating is clearly a part of the skill of managing time. As you plan your day and set priorities, repeatedly ask yourself, "Who else can do this?" The most harried and hurried supervisors are often those people who insist on handling all details themselves.

Delegation Practices

Here are some pointers on the art of delegation:

1. Review your daily plans, checking those items you can assign or delegate to others.
2. Assign as many tasks as you can. At the beginning, expect and accept some mistakes.
3. Give the person enough authority to complete the assignment.
4. Let other persons affected know to whom the task has been delegated.
5. Call for progress reports and schedule reviews on your calendar.
6. Delegate by the results you expect—what you want done rather than what people should do. Permit leeway in the methods used to get things done.

7. Learning to delegate takes repeated practice, too. Pick just one of your present routine duties. Designate someone to handle it for you.

8. Follow through carefully using the suggestions listed here. Then, repeat the process with other time-burdening duties.

HOW TO CONCENTRATE ON THE PROBLEM AT HAND

The frantic rush from problem to problem usually solves few of them but drains a lot of energy. Some interruptions cannot be controlled; however, many apparent interruptions stem from supervisors' efforts to juggle a dozen balls in the air at once.

Skill Developers

To avoid distracting pressures, develop the ability to concentrate intently on the problem at hand.

Let the days come at you one at a time. Resolve to do the best you can each day without thinking anxiously about what lies ahead or worrying over past decisions. (Anxiety and worry are both nonproductive activities and get in the way of getting things done!)

Try to remain calm. Avoid impatience, anger, and irritation as much as you can. These emotions not only slow you down but also rub off on others on whom you depend.

Deal decisively with the problem of the moment. Many supervisors waste time shuffling paperwork instead of dealing with each piece of paper once and for all. As one manager put it, "I always had a scramble of paper on my desk until I laid the law down to myself. Now, I take definite action on each paper that comes across my desk—and on that day." The secret: Do it now.

Work on your toughest tasks—the ones requiring the most concentration and imagination—when you are at your best. The peak energy period varies from individual to individual. Try to determine when you do your best work and adjust your schedule accordingly.

HOW TO FINISH ON TIME

You will find that most jobs can be finished sooner and with less wasted motion if realistic deadlines are set. Some projects carry their own built-in deadlines: production schedules, budgets, end-of-month reports. Many other assignments do not unless you assign them. Do not set unobtainable goals. Learn to know your capacity. With practice, you should be able to say to yourself, "This is something I should be able to finish before I go home tonight."

Skill Exercise

Practice setting deadlines for yourself.

Use your daily planning sheet as a guide.

Check and recheck your accomplishment of deadlines set.

When a deadline is not met, analyze why.

As a supervisor, you are selling something. Your company is buying your services and your time—not the hours you put in, but rather what you put into those hours and can show for your efforts.

Every manager, regardless of what level he or she may be in an organization, begins with the same amount of time. Time is the most precious asset a person has. Not having enough time can cause frustrations and worry and can result in poor performance. The first exercise gives you a chance to examine how you are using this most valuable commodity.

The application exercise you will complete is the same kind of exercise that many corporate executives have done. It should give you valuable insights into how you are spending your work time.

Assignment

During the next week, develop a daily planning sheet listing the major activities you are doing. At the end of the week, examine and list the weaknesses you discover. As in all of the application exercises, you are encouraged to discuss the activity with your supervisor.

ANALYZING YOUR TIME:
SKILL-BUILDING APPLICATION WORKSHEET
Activities In Each Work Hour

	Monday	Tuesday	Wednesday	Thursday	Friday
HOUR 1					
HOUR 2					
HOUR 3					
HOUR 4					
HOUR 5					
HOUR 6					
HOUR 7					
HOUR 8					
HOUR 9					
HOUR 10					

THINGS TO ACCOMPLISH TODAY

In analyzing your time more effectively, it becomes important that you examine daily what you want to accomplish. A helpful technique is to categorize your activities into: Must accomplish, Should accomplish, and Can accomplish items. Set priorities within each of these categories: What is the number one item you want to accomplish, what is the number two item, and so on.

	Priorities 1, 2, 3, etc.	Activity to Accomplish
Must Do	1. 2. 3. 4. 5.	
Should Do	1. 2. 3. 4. 5.	
Can Do	1. 2. 3. 4. 5.	

Work on Must-Do Items First

ANALYZING YOUR ACCOMPLISH LIST

Carefully examine your things-to-accomplish list. Answer these two questions:

1. Were the Must-Do priorities accomplished? Why?

    _____

    _____

    _____

    _____

    _____

    _____

    _____

2. Were the Must-Do priorities not accomplished? Why not?

    _____

    _____

    _____

    _____

    _____

    _____

Ask yourself these three questions:

1. Do I need to spend more concentrated time on Must-Do priorities?
2. Am I spending too much time on the easy items? Remember: Do the tough ones first!!
3. Look for big blocks of time. Do I need to delegate some of the items?

IDEAS FOR IMPROVEMENT

From what you have learned in this chapter unit, list one or more specific actions that you intend to initiate within the next thirty days.

1. _____

_____

_____

_____

_____

_____

_____

2. _____

_____

_____

_____

_____

_____

_____

3. _____

_____

_____

_____

_____

_____

_____

_____

REVIEW QUESTIONS

1. T F People who are successful in managing time tell us that some basic skills are involved that can be learned.
2. T F One important skill necessary is to find the time to plan.
3. T F If you wish to plan your time well, you must develop a complex plan.
4. T F Most people will do the disagreeable or unpleasant tasks first.
5. _____ In setting priorities you visualize a target with three rings of a bull's eye. When a problem arises that needs immediate attention, do you choose:
   (a) Can-be-done ring
   (b) Should-be-done ring
   (c) Must-be-done ring
6. A supervisor, lead person, or key operator repeatedly asks, "Who else can do this?" In management, this is called the skill of _____.
7. The text lists at least four ways to help develop the ability to concentrate on the problems at hand. List three of these ideas.

   _____

   _____

   _____

8. Assume that a person making $5.00/hour loses 30 minutes each working day through poor time management. What is the annual dollar loss impact on one such employee? _____
   What is the annual dollar loss impact on 100 employees?

   _____

9. What do these facts tell you about managing time?

   _____

   _____

10. Estimate the dollar loss impact in your own work group using your rate of pay as average and assuming only five minutes lost per day. Your estimate: _____.

CHAPTER 3

Skill in Planning

Do you run your job or does your job run you? Skill in planning not only enables you to run your job, it also develops your ability to get results. Getting results will mean advancement for yourself and will help you make a major contribution to the successful operation of your department and company.

This chapter is for the reader who wants to improve his or her skills both in day-to-day and long-range planning. Consider the following questions. Compare the answers below with your own thinking and experience.

Question: To what extent does a factory or office supervisor use planning in her daily work?

Answer: Every time work is assigned to employees, material requisitioned, or a job order initiated, some form of planning is required. This means that the supervisor probably plans more times a day than does any other level of management person.

Question: Why, then, does the supervisor need to improve her planning skill?

Answer: The kind of planning a supervisor most frequently does is one-time, on-the-spot planning. The results are normally evident within minutes or hours. The kind of planning skill that needs sharpening deals with longer-term goals and with a greater variety of larger departmental problems.

Question: In what areas should a supervisor do a better planning job?

Answer: Here are five examples:

1. Planning for the training or development needs of employees.
2. Planning for cost improvement in specific areas such as waste, labor efficiency, and equipment maintenance.
3. Planning changes in processes or quality techniques.
4. Participating in planning budgets and setting goals.
5. Planning clerical operations.

Question: Do the advantages that result really justify the time used in thorough planning?

Answer: Yes, in most cases. The real purpose of planning is twofold:

1. To avoid overlooking details that should be considered before action is taken.
2. To coordinate and schedule actions properly so that efforts are placed where there is the most room for improvement.

Question: Is planning ahead merely guesswork and theorizing?

Answer: No; this is a common misconception. Actually, proper planning must be based on the most practical, down-to-earth facts about the past and present, with carefully thought-out estimates of the future.

CHALLENGE OF PLANNING

Planning is essentially a supervisory function. A small amount of time spent in planning or advance thinking on supervisory problems is well repaid.

The development of skill in planning is a great challenge for these three reasons:

1. It is gratifying to see your plan carried to a successful conclusion.

2. Planning for an unknown future can be mentally stimulating.
3. An important qualification for reaching higher management levels is the ability to plan effectively.

This chapter will show how you can develop the specific skills of good planning and how good planning can be successfully carried out.

HOW TO DEVELOP SPECIFIC PLANNING SKILLS

Planning requires the full use of certain specific skills. Look at some of these skills and practice them in order to sharpen your ability to plan.

Skill in Setting an Objective

Why plan? What should you plan? Where should you start? Planning is not just a mental or paperwork exercise. There must be an end to be achieved, a problem to be overcome, or a project to be accomplished. In fact, most successful planning starts with performance that requires improvement in a particular area.

Practice Technique

Select the three biggest problems in your own department. One might be a cost problem; another, a human relations problem; and a third, a quality problem. When you have selected your most pressing problems and determined the results desired, you have set some important planning objectives.

Skill in Forecasting the Future

How can you know what to expect? What will happen tomorrow, or six months hence?

Fundamentally, *planning* is thinking ahead. Therefore, sound judgment is required to estimate what the future facts will be. Much planning that goes astray results from mistaken judgment about the future. A good plan can be devised only when future requirements are known and future events are forecast.

Practice Technique

Forecasting ability can be improved by practice. In your department, forecast each month such statistics as are listed below. One month later, check the actual facts against your forecasts:

1. The average number of people who will be absent daily.
2. The total volume of output that will be produced.
3. The number of service installations that will be completed.
4. The number of mailings that will go out.
5. Which employees will make effective quality improvements.

If these examples are not appropriate for your industry or business, select some that are meaningful for you. On your forecast sheet, note the date one month from today when you will check your results.

Skill in Preparing a Plan

What form should your plan take? How far in the future can you plan? How much detail is needed?

A plan must fit the need. For instance, a simple plan might just be a listing of things to be accomplished, with priorities indicated. A more complicated plan might include detailed analysis of figures, responsibilities of individuals, and different alternatives based on varying future conditions. A plan should be detailed only for the length of time that the future is reasonably predictable. Above all, any plan should include specific target dates for accomplishment.

Practice Technique

Select any item on which you are presently spending more money than the budget permits. Then plan with these four facts in mind:

1. specific causes for the overage
2. steps needed to improve each cause
3. people who must be called on for action
4. specific target dates for each action

Organizing these four factors will result in an effective plan.

Skill in Including Other
People

Should you plan alone? Who, above or below your level, should participate?

Only the simplest plans can be formulated entirely alone. Other people usually must be brought into planning either at the beginning or at a later stage. As a general rule, anyone who will have an important part in carrying out the plan should help in its preparation. However, some thinking and preliminary planning should first be done alone in order to give proper direction and leadership to the planning operation. The following Practice Technique describes a method for identifying all those persons whom you should contact during your planning.

Practice Technique

Prepare a three-column sheet. In the first column, list the steps to be taken in the plan. In the second, list all the people who will be affected. In the third, indicate people who should be included in the planning operation itself. Use this sheet as you proceed with your plan.

CASES THAT WORK

Planning and doing are separate parts of the same job: they are not separate jobs. There is no work that can be performed effectively unless it contains elements of both.[1]

Too often, good planning does not produce the desired results. Why? Because planning must be carried out successfully. It is too easy to feel that the job is done when the planning phase is completed.

Here are some situations in which supervisors not only planned well, but also made sure that their plans worked out.

Planning—for Tomorrow

Supervisor Bill Simpson faced the common problem of not being able to accomplish enough in one day. He decided to work out a system that he later called "Planning for Tomorrow." First, he sat down with a paper and

1. Peter F. Drucker, *Practice of Management.*

pen and listed all the things that had to be done every day. Next, he indicated beside these items the time of day each could definitely be finished. Finally, he decided to list the day before all special items that had to be done "tomorrow."

This plan worked. At first, he had difficulty sticking to his schedule. But after making a few revisions, he found that he could accomplish more by holding himself to completing certain tasks by certain times.

Common Pitfall

Letting the demands of the moment outweigh your plans for an entire day. By consistency and perseverance, you can overcome this problem.

Planning—for Permanent Control

The General Office of Specialty Manufacturing Company always had a varying backlog behind the different sections. As a result, the flow of work bogged down and extra costs crept in.

Department Manager Ray Prentice decided to work out a program for permanently controlling the problem. After initially planning the steps he felt needed to be taken, he discussed his ideas with his three subgroup supervisors to get their ideas and to hear their suggestions for improving the plan. He then submitted the plan to his boss (who had previously held his job) for his advice and subsequent approval. After the changes were made, Ray was able to bring about the improvements he sought, which resulted in cost savings and better flow of work.

Common Pitfalls

Supervisors may sometimes try to 'go it alone' in their plans. Whenever possible, use other persons' knowledge and ideas—especially those of persons who will be directly affected by the plans and whose cooperation is essential to the success of the plan. Not only do you draw on a wider experience base, but you also build in the support and cooperation you need. (Ray consulted both his subordinates and his superior. He probably would have had a more difficult time implementing his plan without the cooperation of both.)

Planning—to Meet a Cost Goal

Like many other companies, State Light and Power faced rising labor costs. Steve Marky's department had a goal of saving 14 percent of the year's labor costs.

Steve had required daily reports from his people and scheduled a weekly planning meeting to discuss specific projects. These meetings included some of his own people plus staff people whose attendance he had arranged.

For two months the goal was met; but then some members of the committee began to lose interest. Steve found it necessary to follow up with these people more frequently than at the weekly meeting. Also, in order to maintain their continued interest he sold them on trying to beat the original 14 percent goal. As a result, he managed to meet this year-end savings goal.

Common Pitfall

When planning extends over a long period of time, it is difficult to maintain a consistent effort. Steve Marky found this out and took steps to prevent the plans from failing.

PARTICIPATING IN THE PLANS OF OTHER PEOPLE

A supervisor has an important managerial responsibility when asked to participate in planning being done by other people. Certain specialized skills are involved in this kind of planning participation.

Indicate Willingness to Participate

Too many group planning efforts are destroyed by the unwilling or indifferent attitude of one member. Even if you are not enthusiastic about participating, try to get as involved as possible. You may surprise yourself and start to enjoy the activity.

Make Constructive Contributions

Planning with other people requires a great deal of give and take. The individual who can give constructively is a most valued participant. Do all you can to keep on the subject. Check to see that you are not displaying any disruptive behavior. Once the meeting has started, do not leave except in a true emergency. Try not to take part in any side conversations or conversations that do not bear directly on what is being discussed.

Carry Out Planning Assignments

When a group is formed to do a planning job, members usually are given assignments and required to report back. For plans to move ahead and to be completed on time, every assignment must be done thoroughly by the required date. If you are given such an assignment, do not be the one who holds up progress.

Make Plans Work

Often a supervisor who participates in planning becomes the person who must eventually carry out the plan. The more of yourself that you have in the plan, the easier it will be for you to give your whole-hearted support to its objectives. Conscientious participation in planning carries an obligation to be equally conscientious in making plans work.

SKILL IN PLANNING:
SKILL-BUILDING APPLICATION

The following four exercises will give you practice in applying planning techniques. The first exercise is on setting planning objectives; the second on practicing forecasting, thinking ahead; and the third is to include other people in your planning. The fourth exercise allows you to put these techniques together into developing a simple but meaningful plan.

SETTING PLANNING OBJECTIVES

To begin to set planning objectives, it is helpful to think of your specific work group/department. These problems may include production, people, or communications, for example.

	SELECT THREE MOST PRESSING PROBLEMS IN YOUR WORKGROUP	LIST THE DESIRED RESULTS YOU WISH TO OBTAIN ON EACH
Problem No. 1		
Problem No. 2		
Problem No. 3		

PRACTICE FORECASTING

In your specific work group, forecast some activities and events that you observe regularly, such as the total volume of your section, the number of people absent daily, or the number of complaints from customers. Make your forecast for one month and then check it with actual results at the end of the month.

ITEM TO BE FORECAST	YOUR PREDICTION	ACTUAL RESULTS (One Month Later)

How did your predictions compare to actual results? Forecasting ability can improve with practice.

PEOPLE PLANNING

Only the simplest plans can be entirely formulated alone. Learn to use people who will have an important part in carrying out a specific plan. In this exercise, list in column one the steps that are to be taken in a plan. In the middle column, list all of the people who are affected; and in the third column, narrow this list to include the people who will help you in carrying out the plan.

LIST THE PLANNING STEPS TO BE TAKEN	LIST THE PEOPLE AFFECTED	LIST THE PEOPLE TO BE INCLUDED IN THE PLANNING PROCESS

PLANNING: APPLICATION

Every supervisor is responsible for planning. Unfortunately, many supervisors and many companies do not fulfill their planning responsibilities; they give as an excuse that they do not have time or that they do not see the value in planning.

Both of these excuses are invalid. With good planning, we are able to free up valuable time and to concentrate on the vital areas of our job. We need to sharpen our planning skills. In this exercise, we will learn how to set good objectives and to implement the steps in the planning process.

Assignment:

Develop a simple plan for improving an individual job problem. (You can probably use one of the problems you identified on the Setting Planning Objectives form.)

PLANNING WORKSHEET

1. Setting Objectives
    A. Identify an individual job problem.

    _____

    _____

    _____

    _____

    _____

    B. Determine the desired results.

    _____

    _____

    _____

    _____

    _____

2. Forecasting the Future
    A. Identify statistical or measurable data surrounding this objective (i.e., costs, volume, downtime, accidents)

    _____

    _____

    _____

    _____

    _____

    B. Check actual figures with what you have projected or forecast.

    _____

    _____

    _____

    _____

    _____

3. Preparing a Plan   (Incorporate these six questions.)

What is to be done? _____

_____

_____

_____

Why is it to be done? _____

_____

_____

_____

When is it to be done? _____

_____

_____

_____

Where is it to be done? _____

_____

_____

_____

Who is to do it? _____

_____

_____

_____

How is it to be done? _____

_____

_____

_____

4. Including Other People   (As a general rule, include in the preparation of the plan anyone who will have an important part in carrying out the plan.)

_____

_____

_____

_____

_____

IDEAS FOR IMPROVEMENT

From what you have learned in this chapter, list one or more specific actions that you intend to initiate within the next thirty days.

1. _____

_____

_____

_____

_____

2. _____

_____

_____

_____

_____

3. _____

_____

_____

_____

_____

REVIEW QUESTIONS

1.   The kind of planning we most frequently do is: (a) on-the-spot planning, (b) daily and weekly planning, or (c) long-range planning.

2.   T   F   The kind of planning skill that needs sharpening is the skill that deals with longer-term goals.

3.   Several areas were discussed in which supervisors should do a better job. List at least three of these areas.

_____

_____

_____

_____

4.   List the four skills helpful in sharpening your planning ability.

_____

_____

_____

_____

5.   T   F   In setting an objective, there must be an end to be achieved, a problem to be overcome, or a project to be accomplished.

6.   T   F   In forecasting the future, we simply have to think ahead and use enough sound judgment to estimate what the future facts will be.

7.   Above everything else, we should include _____

_____

_____ in preparing a plan.

8.   T   F   In including other people as a skill, a general rule should be to include anyone who will have an important part in carrying out the plan.

9.   In each of the three case studies, a common pitfall in planning was identified. List these common pitfalls.

_____

_____

_____

_____

10.   As you look at your own area of work and responsibility, where do you see the need for additional improved planning?

_____

_____

_____

_____

_____

_____

_____

_____

_____

_____

CHAPTER 4

Skill in Decision Making

You have probably heard someone say, "I don't mind my job—it is just all those decisions I have to make." Actually, it is how you reach your decisions, minute-by-minute and day-by-day, that makes your job pleasant or nerve racking, easy or hard, a success or a failure.

This chapter will help you as supervisors to improve your own skills in a most important area of managerial ability—making decisions.

ALL THOSE DECISIONS . . .

If you think back over the work day, you can probably recall five or six important decisions you have made. In fact, a supervisor makes many more than that—possibly as many as fifty or more a day. This number may sound high, but it includes decisions of a wide variety and type. Each decision affects the performance of the operations he supervises.

People or Things

Some decisions primarily concern people. Other decisions concern things. Of course, most decisions are a combination of both people and things.

Self or Others

You may generally think of decisions involving other people. But equally important are decisions made on the job regarding yourself. For instance, whether to spend two hours, or a half-hour, on a particular problem, may be an important decision.

Big or Little

The big decisions are easily remembered. The little ones are frequently not even thought of as decisions. Yet, the decisions to correct an employee, to assign one piece of work ahead of another, to recommend action to your superior may all be little decisions that have a big effect on performance. *Every time you make a choice, every time you take action, you have made a decision.* Big or little, each decision is an important factor in your managerial effectiveness.

THE DECISION-MAKING PROCESS

To understand the decision-making process is not easy. This process is characterized by four seeming contradictions:

1. Decisions should be based on facts; but frequently, not all the facts are available.
2. In making decisions, it is important to be objective, unbiased, unemotional. Yet sound decisions are based on an accurate analysis of other people's emotions and reactions.
3. Decisions become precedents for future decisions, but any decision must be based in part on previous decisions.
4. A decision always involves risk, but making no decision also involves risk.

Yes, the decision-making process is complex, but not so complicated that you cannot master it. In this chapter, we will dig beneath the decision-making process. In addition, we will suggest some fundamental Practice Techniques to help you improve your decision-making skill.

HOW TO DEVELOP DECISION-MAKING SKILLS

Skill in making sound decisions really involves the effective use of a number of fundamental management skills. Different skills are used in each of the Basic Steps that are followed in making a decision.

As you think about some of the skills discussed, decide in which of these skills you are the strongest, and in which the weakest. Then, conscientiously use the Practice Techniques to improve your weaker skills in order to improve your overall decision-making ability.

Step 1. Setting Practical Goals

Every decision is based on some goal or objective whether known to all employees or a goal in the mind of the decision maker. Therefore, it is of primary importance that goals be clear and attainable. Otherwise, individual decisions will seem vague and indefinite to employees, and several decisions taken together may seem inconsistent or unfair.

The skills necessary for setting practical goals require:

1. The ability to interpret top management decisions, which really form the basic goals for your activities or operations.
2. The ability to translate management goals into departmental job objectives. These objectives fall into two areas. First, overall quotas, expressed in dollars, quantities, or other figures. Second, standards of performance for employees, including the human relations practices and attitudes that you think are important.

Practice Techniques

When you have time to yourself, use a pen and paper on the following practice steps.

1. Write down six to ten departmental goals, some of which are quotas and some of which are performance standards.
2. Jot down specific decisions you have made to attain each goal.
3. Rate your progress to date on these goals. Starting with "1," indicate in order the areas in which progress has been greatest.

4. Look over your rating. Necessary areas for decision and action will quickly come to mind.

Guiding Principle

Too many decisions are made under crisis conditions. By setting practical goals, decisions can be made before trouble arises. Furthermore, keeping these goals strongly in mind should prevent decisions that would block progress.

Step 2. Recognizing the Problem and Finding Facts

Recognizing the real problem—not just grabbing what may be a surface problem—is the core of decision making. Finding the problem will lead logically to the required facts; and a good job of fact-finding usually (but not always) points the way to the best decision.

The skills required to improve your fact-finding skill include developing:

1. Capacity for acute observation and alertness to conditions that indicate possible problems in advance.
2. Ability to formulate in your own mind a clear statement of the basic problem.
3. Power to concentrate and stubbornly track down facts. The question-asking process requires toughness—not toward people—but with respect to accuracy of information.

Practice Techniques

Two practice drills are suggested here. Written or mental, each drill should become a permanent part of your approach to every decision.

1. Select a problem you presently have, one on which no decision has yet been made. Before getting the facts, list what facts you feel you need, without prejudging whether you can get them or not. Note how many facts you have listed. How many might you have forgotten, had you plunged into the fact-finding step without a few minutes of planning?
2. Proceed to get all the available facts. Write down the facts you do not have that you feel you need. Next to each important missing fact, write down the best assumption you can make. Exploring these facts and assumptions gives you a basis for decision making.

Use judgment in determining the right amount of time to spend on fact gathering. Learn to preplan the problem-recognition and fact-finding steps. Such planning will lead to an overall grasp of the situation and also will prevent missing the point.

Step 3. Decision and Action

Decision making is more than merely adding up advantages and disadvantages. More often than not, making decisions involves considering unlike elements, such as cost-saving on the one hand, versus employee attitudes on the other.

Practically speaking, decision making is a process of eliminating alternatives, each of which may have some degree of merit.

The skills required to reach a decision include:

1. Keen insight into how people and things work, plus intelligent foresight into how people and things will react to change.
2. Open-mindedness in approaching the main alternative actions that present themselves. Seldom does only one feasible solution far outweigh all others.
3. A good sense of timing action. The decision that was sound a week ago may not be the decision that is advisable today.

Practice Techniques

Some people spend too much time mulling over many alternatives. But more common is the tendency to jump to a conclusion or quickly close the mind to all but one alternative. Practice the following technique whenever possible:

Put down on paper all the possible alternative decisions to a problem without evaluating them in advance.

Brainstorm the problem, attempting to see how many courses of action you can find.

Later, come back and make a decision.

Guiding Principle

Selecting a course of action requires all the intelligence and experience you can muster. Sound, effective decisions rarely can be made off the top of the head. They come from hard, careful thought, whether they are made quickly or slowly.

COMBINING SKILLS

The overall skill to make sound decisions involves the combination of many varied specific skills.

Setting practical objectives requires the ability to plan ahead and to anticipate operational needs.

Getting the facts demands concentration and efficiency in using valuable time.

Selecting the right decision requires basic intelligence in balancing a number of unlike facts.

Perhaps the greatest decision-making skill that a manager can acquire is the ability to know when a decision can be made on the spot, and when it is better to walk away to think first.

SKILL IN DECISION MAKING:
SKILL-BUILDING APPLICATION
SETTING PRACTICAL GOALS

Every decision is based on some goal or objective. Therefore, for decisions to be clear and definite, it is important that goals be clear and attainable. Think of your departmental goals and complete the following exercise. The goals may be either quotas or some performance standard for you or your people.

LIST AT LEAST THREE GOALS OF YOUR WORK GROUP OR DEPARTMENT	DECISION YOU HAVE MADE OR MUST MAKE TO ATTAIN THIS GOAL	CHECK APPROPRIATE PROGRESS TO DATE.		
		EXCELLENT	FAIR	POOR

PROBLEM PROCESSING

Learning to recognize the real problem is the core of good decision making. You may need to learn how to process both the facts and the assumptions you are making about the problem.

Select a problem you presently have, one on which no decision has yet been made.

_____

_____

_____

List the facts you feel you need in order to make a good decision on this problem.

_____

_____

_____

_____

_____

_____

This simple planning exercise may often keep you from plunging off the deep end of a wrong decision.

Remember: in many decisions, assumptions you are making are as important as facts you are gathering. Carefully analyze your assumptions.

What assumptions are you making about the problem?

_____

_____

_____

_____

_____

_____

APPLICATION

Good decision making is important to a supervisor. It is the key to daily existence. Many times, the available facts may be limited. You may have little past experience to rely on, and yet the decision you must make will have a large impact on the organization.

It is in times like these that you realize the need for a good system to use in the decision process. You can learn the proven steps in making a decision, but these steps must be practiced. Only with practice can the decision-making steps become a part of your daily activity.

The care with which you make decisions and the force with which they are carried out are measures of your effectiveness. Making good decisions requires good *thinking* and *practice.*

DECISION-MAKING WORKSHEET

ASSIGNMENT: Complete this worksheet, working through the decision-making steps listed.

1. List one job goal or objective.

    _____

    _____

    _____

2. List the specific things that you have done to accomplish this goal.

    _____

    _____

    _____

    _____

    _____

    _____

3. Identify necessary problem or action areas.

    _____

    _____

    _____

4. Gather the available facts that you feel are necessary concerning this problem or action area.

    _____

    _____

    _____

5. List possible alternative decisions to help you solve this problem.

    _____

    _____

    _____

6. Choose the best decision for the problem based on what you have learned. (Make mental notes of your success ratio of this and future decisions so that you can more accurately continue to make meaningful decisions.) Good decision making simply means improving your decision-making batting average.

_____

_____

_____

_____

_____

_____

IDEAS FOR IMPROVEMENT

From what you have learned in this chapter, list one or more specific actions that you intend to initiate within the next thirty days.

1. _____
   _____
   _____
   _____
   _____

2. _____
   _____
   _____
   _____
   _____

3. _____
   _____
   _____
   _____
   _____

REVIEW QUESTIONS

1.   List the one item that you feel causes you the most problem in making decisions.

        _____

2. T   F   Every time you make a choice, every time you take action, you have made a decision.

3. T   F   Every decision is based on some goal or objective, whether it is known to all employees or whether a goal is in the mind only of the person making the decision.

4.   Within a company, the goals and objectives normally fall into two areas: quotas and standards of performance. Within your own company, list a goal that relates to quotas.

        _____

5.   Within your company, list a goal that relates to standards of performance of employees.

        _____

6.   The core of decision making is to recognize the _____

        _____.

7. T   F   Sound decisions for many people come very quickly off the top of their head.

8. T   F   A decision always involves risk.

9. T   F   No decision always involves risk.

10.   Complete the assignment in the application section by first identifying a job goal or objective you now have. Then proceed through the decision-making steps outlined.

CHAPTER 5

Skill in Communication

I nstructions. Orders. Phone calls. Meetings. Memos. You may spend close to 90 percent of your time sharing information — communicating in some form. With so much practice, you ought to be skilled. Yet every so often you may realize that you have not gotten through to the people you contact daily on the job.

Most supervisory activities involve contacts with other people, and each such contact requires skillful handling of the information-sharing process.

SKILL IN SENDING

Communication can be compared to a radio network. A radio transmitter beams out messages; but if there are no receivers in the vicinity to pick up the messages, communication does not take place. Communication includes both sending and receiving.

This is also true on the job. The supervisor is a source of much information. She 'sends out' facts and instructions. When she issues a directive, either oral or written, she may think she has communicated. But to transmit information effectively her employees must be 'tuned in' to receive it. To build receptiveness in employees requires skill in 'sending'—in memo and report writing, speaking, conference leading, and other related areas.

SKILL IN RECEIVING

Suppose your 'radio station' is sending out messages and they are being picked up, but the listeners do not understand the broadcast because it is in some language they do not know. Again, no communication takes place. Communication implies not only sending and receiving, but also understanding. On the job, the challenge is to master the art of listening in order to grapple with difficult differences in meaning and thus achieve understanding.

THE SCOPE OF COMMUNICATION

A supervisor should be able to represent the company to her subordinates, to answer questions, and to explain policies; at the same time, she should be able to interpret to superiors the thinking of the people in the ranks.

The supervisor is not only concerned with sharing information with her employees. She also is the center of a communications set-up in which communication moves from management to employees and from employees to management. She may exchange ideas with other supervisors, participate in training conferences, and consult with staff people.

In each case, she must know not only what to say, but she also must be able to interpret what the other person is saying. Information flows upward, downward, outward, and inward.

In communication on the job, actions may speak louder than words. Communication is not all language. We use looks, gestures, actions, expressions, attitudes, and even body posture to communicate with others. A supervisor's scowl, a shrug of the shoulders, or a smile may convey a meaning, intended or otherwise, more significant than words. You probably have heard it said, "Your actions speak so loudly that I cannot hear a word you say."

With practice and drill, a supervisor can become increasingly skillful in handling on-the-job communications. Apply the practice pointers, tips, and suggestions on the following pages as part of your own self-development program.

HOW TO DEVELOP COMMUNICATION SKILL

Words are tools by which ideas and thoughts are exchanged. When skillfully used, words exert a powerful influence on the thoughts and actions of the people who hear them.

The Communication Process

To master the skills of information-sharing, you should first have a clear picture of what happens, or *should* happen, when you communicate. Five rather distinct activities can be identified in the process of information-sharing.

1. *Plan* your approach: decide how to share information.
2. *Explain* what you mean: express yourself clearly.
3. *Listen* to understand: search for the real meaning of what the other person says.
4. *Verify* by playback: double-check what the other person means.
5. *Evaluate* through follow-up: be sure that mutual understanding has been achieved.

Communication may be thought of as an exchange of information in which meaning is alternately expressed, received, repeated, and assimilated until there is a complete meeting of the minds.

Even though planning should precede any communication initiated by the supervisor, it is obvious that communication may also start at some other point. For example, if the employee comes up to you and begins to blast with both barrels, you are immediately on the listening or receiving end of the conversation, with no time to plan. But before having your say, you can proceed to verify and evaluate.

The following practice drills can help you develop skill in communication activities.

HOW TO PLAN YOUR APPROACH

All too often, communication breaks down before it really begins — at the planning stage. The urge to be decisive and efficient should not trap you into short cutting careful planning.

Planning Pointers

To develop skill in planning your communications, practice with this paper-and-pencil drill. Before relaying information or discussing a problem, jot down the answers to these questions:

1. Exactly what do I want to accomplish by communicating?
2. What information do I want to relay?
3. What additional information should I draw out during the course of discussion?
4. How well do I know the persons with whom I will be talking? What values, goals, interests, and opinions are they likely to bring to the conversation?
5. How will I introduce the subject and what do I plan to say?
6. When is the best time to communicate?

HOW TO EXPLAIN WHAT YOU MEAN

If your associates or employees do not understand what you are talking about, your communication has not succeeded. So, when you put yourself on the air, be sure you are getting your message across to your audience.

Talking Tips

Follow these suggestions when you are talking:

1. Try to use words that will have the same meaning for both you and your listener. (To a worker in your shop, *fringe* may mean extra payroll benefits; to a fashion designer it may be a decoration on a shawl. *Diamond* may mean a baseball field to a sports fan; but to a newly engaged couple it may mean a ring.)
2. Avoid fuzzy phrases such as *work harder,* or *take it easy.* Instead,

be specific: "Jerry, you must increase your production by 10 percent this week." Or, "Take your coffee break and calm down. We will discuss this matter at two o'clock in my office."

3. Recognize that your actions, or lack of action, also convey meaning.

4. Consider your tone of voice. Does it get across to the listener the meaning you intend?

5. Avoid unnecessary details.

6. Identify the subject you plan to talk about.

7. Arouse listener interest.

HOW TO LISTEN

The next time you are engaged in a conversation, try to analyze what you do while other people are speaking. Are you really attentive, or do you find your thoughts wandering to other subjects? Are you thinking ahead to what you will say next? Do you find yourself fighting for the floor?

Perhaps the most difficult communication skill to acquire is the art of listening. The more a supervisor practices and becomes adept at listening, the more she becomes convinced that listening itself can be a persuasive device.

Suggestions

As a listener, your aim should be to understand what the sender is trying to say, not what you *think* the sender has in mind. Here are some suggestions for improving listening skills:

1. Do not jump to conclusions. Do not assume or anticipate anything. Do not let the speaker think you know what will come next.

2. Try to understand the speaker's objective—the real reason behind the effort to communicate with you.

3. Give the other person enough time to complete his or her thoughts. Do not interrupt.

4. Do not react immediately to what the speaker says. Your first reaction may not be correct. A word that the speaker uses may not have the same meaning for both of you. If something that is said does not make sense, then consider some alternative definitions.

Listening is not a time for relaxation or daydreaming. It is a time for concentration and thoughtful effort in order to understand the meaning the speaker is trying to convey.

HOW TO VERIFY BY FEEDBACK

The listener should not interrupt, but there is need to verify and clarify your understanding of what the speaker has said. This step in the communication process is not complete until the speaker knows that the two parties have reached agreement. They should, however, thoroughly understand any areas of disagreement.

Feedback Pointers

The feedback technique can be used by the listener to verify meaning. In *feedback*, you restate in your own words what has been said by the other party. For example, "As I understand it, Billie, you would rather not take on this shift assignment." Or, you may need to probe for unexpressed ideas; "Let's go over that again, Mary. I want to be sure I understand what you have in mind." Or again, you may find it necessary to ask specific factual questions, such as "What deductions were made from your last pay check, Fran?"

During this phase of the discussion, the listener should not make statements or attempt to provide answers. The very fact that a sincere effort is being made to understand often paves the way to a change in the other person's outlook.

SKILL IN COMMUNICATION: ROLE-PLAY APPLICATIONS

One of the most effective ways to improve communications is to learn to use the technique of practicing and trying an approach on someone you know and respect. You can learn greatly through this approach of role playing.

Practice role playing the following two situations. To gain most from this approach, be honest and use conversation and examples that you would be likely to use in a real situation. After the role playing, critically review what you thought were the strengths and weaknesses of your approach.

PRACTICE SESSIONS

1. If, in the near future, you plan to *explain* a company policy, a change in specifications, an overtime assignment, a work methods revision, or some other matter to any employee, try out your explanation ahead of time. Ask another supervisor to assume the role of the employee— assuming the same attitude, asking the same kinds of questions an employee would probably raise in an actual situation. Try to make the conversation as close to the real thing as possible instead of discussing it as one supervisor to another. This technique will give you an advance sample of the kind of reaction you might expect to meet in dealing with a face-to-face communication problem.

2. A practice session in *listening* will help accustom you to the habit of hearing out the other person. Such a session may be played with another supervisor representing the employee with a complaint or grievance, with your spouse or a friend in the role of an unhappy customer, or with some other person on the staff of your organization taking the part of an employee with a suggestion for a job methods improvement. It might be best to find another supervisor with an interest in improving his or her communication-sharing techniques. You can play the guinea pig for each other. Ralph Waldo Emerson once stated:

> Do not say things. What you are stands over you the while and thunders so that I cannot hear what you say to the contrary.

Communication is the art of transmitting thoughts, feelings, and ideas from one person to another. The following chapters will examine several methods of communications, including: "Talking Effectively,"

"Reading, Memo and Report Writting," and "Selling Your Ideas." And, as Emerson has stated so well, you will observe actions. As you examine each of these communication skills, you can practice the process of good communications and learn how to avoid many of the common pitfalls.

SKILL IN COMMUNICATIONS:
SKILL-BUILDING APPLICATION
COMMUNICATIONS CHECKLIST

(You should be able to answer every question "Yes," if you are prepared for your communications.)

	YES	NO
Plan My Approach		
Do I know exactly what I want to accomplish?	___	___
Do I know what information I want to send?	___	___
Do I know how I am going to start?	___	___
Have I looked at what is the best time?	___	___
Explain What I Mean		
Am I prepared to speak the same language?	___	___
Am I prepared to use clear phrases?		
Have I weeded out unnecessary details?	___	___
Have I examined the tone of my message?	___	___
Listen		
Have I determined the additional information needed to be drawn out?	___	___
Have I practiced the techniques of active listening?	___	___
Verify		
Have I formulated my ideas so that I can honestly listen to what is said and so that I can play back information accurately?	___	___
Am I prepared not to interrupt?	___	___
Evaluate		
Am I observing indications of communications other than by the words being expressed?	___	___
Am I aware of the attitudes that are also being communicated?	___	___

IDEAS FOR IMPROVEMENT

From what you have learned in this chapter, list one or more specific actions that you intend to initiate within the next thirty days.

1. _____

   _____

   _____

   _____

   _____

   _____

2. _____

   _____

   _____

   _____

   _____

   _____

3. _____

   _____

   _____

   _____

   _____

   _____

REVIEW QUESTIONS

1. T   F   Managerial success awaits the supervisor who can develop workable skills in communciations.

2.   Communications implies not only sending and receiving, but also _____

   _____.

3.   In communications, actions may speak louder than words. Identify at least three ways we communicate by actions.

   _____

   _____

   _____

4.   List the five steps of the communication process.

   _____

   _____

   _____

   _____

   _____

5.   Communications takes much of our time in instructing, giving orders, phone calls, meetings, memos, and other areas. It is estimated we spend approximately _____ percent of our time communicating in some form.

6. T   F   It is very easy to listen; listening is the easiest form of communication known.

7.   One of the main reasons that communication is not effective is that we see too much of (a) one-way communication, (b) two-way communications.

8.   There are many ways we communicate by words, actions, symbols, and attitudes. Which of these methods do you feel is most troublesome for you? _____

   _____

9.   Why do you think that this method is the most difficult
       for you? _____

       _____

10.   Complete the Communications Checklist in the applica-
       tion section before any important communication. It also
       will serve as preparation for the next chapter, "Skill in
       Talking Effectively."

CHAPTER 6

Skill in Talking Effectively

C an you recall when:

One of your employees misunderstood an oral instruction?

A problem was made more confusing because of what someone said?

Time was wasted at a meeting because of a long-winded speaker?

You failed to get acceptance of an idea?

Someone said, "No one ever told me."?

Situations such as these indicate why talking effectively is more than just talking.

Talking effectively is a key to leadership. You have hundreds of occasions to express ideas, to exchange information, to influence attitudes, and to use the spoken word in directing the efforts of people.

This chapter shows you how to improve your talking skill. No person was born with the ability to speak effectively. It is a skill that leaders have learned and developed.

WORDS AROUND US

Like the air you breathe, there is so much talk around that you often may take the skill of talking for granted. From "Good morning" to "See you tomorrow," the work day is filled with words, ideas, thoughts, comments, and questions. Everyone talks, but not everyone talks effectively.

Even though talking comes naturally, mastering and improving this skill opens the door to better understanding between people. Talking effectively adds more significance to every personal contact. It brings about fuller personal satisfaction and self-confidence. It can make the difference between getting results on the job and just putting in another day's work.

WORDS AT WORK

Estimates show that as a supervisor, you speak between ten and twenty thousand words each day. Almost every one of these spoken words can rightly or wrongly affect your department.

Passing Information

Decisions, policies, complaints, suggestions, and bits of information issue from the supervisor. Instructing an employee, reviewing performance, giving assignments, chatting, speaking before groups are all ways of passing information.

Exchanging Ideas

Problem solving and experience sharing are handled in supervisory round-table discussions, staff meetings, or informal get-togethers.

Influencing Ideas

Supervisors get acceptance of ideas and shape attitudes both up and down the line.

Understanding People

Supervisors are involved with their people in talking about grievances, suggestions, instruction, and even in small talk.

By knowing how to talk, a supervisor can multipy herself through others. Words are always at work.

HOW TO DEVELOP YOUR
TALKING SKILL

The famous orator William Jennings Bryan said the ability to speak effectively is an acquirement rather than a gift.

Every day offers many opportunities to improve your talking skill. You can improve and you will improve— *if you practice.*

Face-to-face talking is a vital link in communication. The willingness and ability of the listener to understand, accept, and use what you say is the final test of how effectively you speak.

Practice Pointers

Skill in talking one-to-one will come easier if you remember these six key ideas:

1. Tailor your approach to your listener—who you are talking to and how that person thinks.
2. Look at the listener. You will get attention and hold it.
3. Talk about one thing at a time, rather than jumping around with unrelated ideas.
4. Avoid attacking expressions or quibbling over words, such as saying, "What do you mean, you do not think it is fair?"
5. Do not talk down to people. Never assume they do not know.
6. Pace yourself. When some people ask questions, they are slowing you down so that they can digest and think over what you have said.

Practice Guide

You can learn from experience.

1. Start off by analyzing the last three conversations you have had. Compare the plus side with the minus side.

+	−
You remembered the other person's name.	You cut in on the other person.
The other person seemed to get your point	You did not understand an objection that the other person made.
You did not argue.	The other person's attention wandered.

After conversations have gotten off the track, review them. You can learn from mistakes.

2. An effective talking situation depends, to a considerable degree, on how well you understand the listener. Let us assume you are talking about business conditions with: (a) an older employee; (b) another supervisor; (c) an employee who always complains; (d) a top executive who comes into your department; (e) a visiting sales person.

Use the following Skill Guide. Think of how you would vary your approach in each case. Size up your listener by asking yourself:

How well do I know this person?

What do I know about his or her interests?

How much does each of us know about the subject we are discussing?

Will the listener have preconceived attitudes toward the subject?

What is this person's attitude toward me?

HOW TO PARTICIPATE IN A CONFERENCE

The people in a group participating in a conference are often more responsible for the success of the conference than is the leader. Whether pooling ideas or solving problems, a conference of which you are a member can be productive, rather than wasted, depending on how *you* act and what real contribution *you* make.

Practice Pointers

To improve your mastery of working with people in a group use these seven techniques:

1. Tune up your thinking before the conference by getting certain facts or jotting down questions.
2. If you do not know someone by name, lead off by introducing yourself. By saying, "I am Bo Smith" the other person may respond with, "I am Leslie Brown."
3. Do not hesitate to get into the act. A well-chosen question can help break the ice. Then you can enter into the discussion and speak freely.
4. If anything is to be said, say it to the group. Avoid side comments.
5. Bear in mind that no one came to hear you give speeches on pet ideas and biased opinions.
6. Do not destroy thinking or constructive discussion with a negative attitude ("It cannot be done that way") or by going off on a tangent.
7. Be polite in listening to other people. Settle any differences through negotiation and give-and-take.

Practice Guide

Remember these points:

1. A conference cannot be productive if it is nothing more than an exchange of words. It must produce results. The real payoff comes later through the subsequent actions of the conference members. At the next conference you attend, jot down notes on "Action to be Taken." Then follow through.
2. You will be more alert (and will stay awake) in a group discussion if you wrestle in your mind with each point that is made. Ask questions and add other comments. Keep your ideas and reactions running through your mind. Remember this: the supervisor who takes part in a meeting gets more out of the meeting than one who just takes it all in.

HOW TO TALK ON YOUR FEET

Successful managing calls for explaining policies to a number of employees, instructing a group, talking before other supervisors, and presenting a plan to higher management. As a leader, you must be able to stand on your feet; you must have confidence in yourself when talking before people.

Practice Pointers

When you are getting ready to talk, follow these seven steps for assurance and effectiveness:

SEVEN STEPS TO SUCCESSFUL SPEAKING

1. *Plan:*   Planning is half the battle in making a successful speech. Use a simple outline so you know what to say and so you stay on the track.
2. *Start:*   Most people tighten up before giving a speech, but you should relax and take plenty of time to get started. Give your opening sentence—pause—then get all wrapped up in what you want to say.
3. *Attract Attention:*   With your opening statement, try to get the attention of everyone listening. State the problem, use a quotation, or refer to what someone has said.
4. *Pace Your Delivery:*   Start in low gear and gradually build up your volume. When you come to an important point, you can become more emphatic, pause after stating it, or repeat the idea using other words. Always try to be yourself, rather than imitating a speaker you have heard.
5. *Illustrate:*   Whenever possible, use illustrations to make your point. Use examples, diagrams, visual aids, anecdotes, or draw on the experience of the people who are listening to you.
6. *Sum Up:*   Always try to end with some sort of conclusion or summary of the points you have made.
7. *Stop:*   As the well-known aphorism says, "No soul was ever saved by a sermon that lasted more than twenty minutes." Stop while your listeners are still with you!

A simple, basic formula for giving a talk before a group is: Tell them what you are going to tell them; tell them; tell them what you have told them.

Reading or memorizing a speech can make your talk sound dull and even meaningless. A good technique is to put your outline on 3 × 5 cards for ready reference. Use a different card for each main idea. On the cards, list major headings, subtopics, and key points, rather than entire sentences.

After giving a talk, ask one or two friends who have heard it for their reactions and suggestions. You will probably be surprised to learn how well you did!

Practice Guide

The best way to gain confidence and skill is to *practice.* No speakers were ever developed by reading about speech making. Instead of awarding chances of giving talks, find opportunities to improve your talking while at work or in community activities.

Let us assume that you are going to give a fifteen minute talk to a group of employees about safety. In planning your talk, make up a simple outline:

Purpose

1. To get employees' ideas on accident prevention.
2. To enlist participation in attacking accident causes.

Time

1. You, the supervisor, choose the best time—perhaps beginning or end of a shift.
2. Allow fifteen minutes for discussion.

Place

1. At actual hazard spot.
2. At quiet location, or
3. At your desk, workplace, or office.

Discussion

A. Open the discussion (*Time:* 2 minutes)
    1. Announce purpose: "We want to talk about improving accident prevention."

2. Describe safety problem: "Today, we will talk about our single biggest cause of accidents, which is. . . ."
3. Suggest plan: "First, I have some facts. Then we will discuss our problem. Finally, we will decide action."

B. Present facts (*Time:* 3 minutes)
1. Give credit to employees who have been particularly helpful in improving safety record.

C. Start employee discussion (*Time:* 8 minutes)
1. Ask for improvement ideas. Example: "Billie, do you have any ideas to prevent our biggest accident problem?"
2. Get a second comment on the same idea. Example: "Diane, how does that strike you?"
3. Comment briefly, and get another idea. Example: "Sounds good. I will write it down. Lee, what is another idea for us to think about?"
4. Keep the discussion constructive. Example: "That is a fair criticism, Jo. How can we prevent that in the future?"

D. Summarize
1. Repeat the best ideas.
2. Compliment the group on its discussion.

Whether you are an office or a factory supervisor, you can prepare an outline similar to this one whenever you plan to call a few employees together to discuss a problem or situation of concern to the group.

HOW TO GET ACCEPTANCE OF IDEAS

The skillful supervisor at the outset gets a number of "yes" responses in trying to gain acceptance for her ideas. She sets up a process of moving her listeners in an affirmative train of thought. It is like aiming a bowling ball. You hit one pin, and it knocks the others over.

Practice Pointers

To create acceptance of an idea, keep these practical pointers in mind:

1. Before talking about an idea, jot down key points on paper. Review them so you can be convincing, sincere, and result-getting.
2. Do not try to win arguments. Arguments usually end up with

each contestant more firmly convinced than ever that he or she is right.

3. Simplify figures, specifications, formulas, and technical data. It is better to say, "We can expect a 20 percent savings," than, "Our costs will be reduced from $3,000 to $2,400."

4. Try to anticipate any objections and weave your answers to them into the conversation.

5. When you come to a major point, repeat it more than once, using different words.

6. When a listener looks confused or is not following you, change your pace. Slow down, restate, or ask for a reaction.

7. Use demonstrations or charts. It has been said that the best way to show that a stick is crooked is to lay a straight stick beside it.

Practice Guide

Before presenting an idea, try it out on another person. Even informally reviewing an idea with someone else will help you state it better. A practical pretesting of ideas in this way will help clarify the idea in your own mind.

Dale Carnegie is often remembered for his idea that the people you are talking to are much more interested in themselves and their wants and problems than they are in you and your problems.

Talking Tips

No matter how much knowledge you acquire, no matter how well your mind is disciplined, your public image and accomplishments depend on your ability to express yourself. Skillful talking not only depends on what you say, but also on how you say it and sometimes even on when you say it.

Whenever you talk, make sure you know what you are talking about. Nothing undermines the respect of employees for their supervisors than the feeling that the supervisors are just talking to hear the sound of their own voices.

Talking is a two-way street. It is easy to *tell* someone what to do. It takes much more skill to get real *acceptance.* Listen with both your ears and your brain engaged so you will "hear" what the other person says, thinks, and feels.

Talk the language. Talk to be understood by using words that other people understand. Speak loudly enough so that people can hear. You will not achieve the results you want by using obscure language or talking with marbles in your mouth. Resist the impulse to overstate your case.

Your attitude toward people, problems, and the company shines through in the words you use and by the way you talk.

SKILL IN TALKING EFFECTIVELY: SKILL-BUILDING APPLICATION

As in most every skill, talking fails when we do not positively practice and improve our techniques. Think of an example from your own experience when . . .

Your instructions were totally misunderstood.

_____

_____

_____

_____

_____

_____

Which instructions were misunderstood? Why?

_____

_____

_____

_____

_____

You had to give different sets of instructions to different people in order to get them to do the same thing.

_____

_____

_____

_____

_____

_____

At the end of a meeting or conference the participants went out and did exactly the wrong things.

_____

_____

_____

_____

_____

_____

What would you do differently to keep the same thing from happening again?

_____

_____

_____

_____

_____

_____

_____

_____

_____

_____

APPLICATION

Talking effectively is a key to leadership. It is a skill that successful leaders have learned and developed. But like most skills, it is acquired rather than simply being a gift. The listed skill pointers are vital to developing this key skill.

ASSIGNMENT: Ask to brief your supervisor on a proposal or problem relative to your job or a job you are familiar with in your department.

TALKING EFFECTIVELY
WORKSHEET

1. Prepare a Briefing Plan (List in topical outline the main points of the briefing.)

    A. _____

    _____

    1. _____

    (List subheadings if needed)

    2. _____

    B. _____

    C. _____

2. Prepare Approach   (Choose the best approach with illustrations necessary to enhance your briefing.)

    _____

    _____

    _____

    _____

    _____

    _____

    _____

4. Summarize   (Repeat best idea. Ask for questions.)

_____

_____

_____

_____

_____

_____

_____

_____

IDEAS FOR IMPROVEMENT

From what you have learned in this chapter, list one or more specific actions
that you intend to initiate within the next thirty days.

1. _____

   _____

   _____

   _____

   _____

   _____

2. _____

   _____

   _____

   _____

   _____

   _____

3. _____

   _____

   _____

   _____

   _____

   _____

   _____

   _____

REVIEW QUESTIONS

1. T   F   Talking effectively is a key to leadership that successful people have learned and developed.

2.   Estimates have shown that an average supervisor speaks approximately _____ words per day.

3. T   F   William Jennings Bryan stated that a person has to be given the gift of speaking effectively and that it could not be acquired.

4. T   F   Sometimes it is wise to assume that people do not know and they are not interested; therefore, you must occasionally talk down to these people.

5.   List at least three points that are important to master when your boss asks you to participate in a conference.

_____

_____

_____

_____

6. T   F   A simple basic formulation for summarizing the seven points for getting ready to talk is: tell them what you are going to tell them; tell them; and tell them what you told them.

7. T   F   The best way to gain confidence and skill in speaking is to practice.

8. T   F   It is easy to tell someone what to do, but it takes a more skillful speaker to gain real confidence.

9.   Think of the last conversation or talk that you had in which you had a communications failure. Identify this particular failure area.

_____

_____

_____

_____

10.   Analyze what went wrong based on your understanding of key points discussed in this chapter.

_____

_____

_____

_____

_____

_____

_____

_____

Skill in Memo and Report Writing

Do I habitually postpone and avoid all writing?

Am I self-conscious about my lack of writing ability?

Has a memo to someone ever misfired?

Do I only put things on paper when specifically requested?

Do I get swamped with the details involved in writing?

If your answer is *yes* to any of these questions, then this chapter will help you develop the necessary skills and techniques so that you can talk on paper in an orderly, concise, and competent fashion. It will make it possible for your ideas to get better attention and consideration.

WHY WRITE?

Industrial managers, top executives, office managers, and department heads are all spending more and more of their time accumulating facts and passing them on with their own comments and conclusions. In the past, most information was transferred by word of mouth. Today, a busy executive has less time to listen to oral reports. She prefers to have certain facts on paper. As time goes on, the ability to present ideas on paper may mean the difference between getting that promotion you have been looking for, or watching it go to someone else.

ORGANIZED THOUGHT

Writing reports, whether routine or special, is part of every supervisor's job. Well-written reports save the time of everyone who reads them. Further, they assist you in the decision-making process because the orderly process involved in writing a report helps you organize your thoughts and analyze the issues involved.

In large companies, the only means of communication between certain people may be by the exchange of memos or reports. In all companies, it is important to realize that your ability as a supervisor may be judged by the written information you submit.

SIMPLE APPROACH

We have all seen written instructions misfire because they failed to reach the reader. Getting the point across is best accomplished with a few short words and simple sentences. Big words and complicated sentences lay a smoke screen over the real ideas you are selling. And, make no mistake, some of your best selling can be done on paper.

YOUR REPORT IS YOU

Memos, reports, and letters should be constructive. They must keep the main purpose in mind and not rehash old issues. They must be thought-provoking to the reader, yet reflect your viewpoint. Finally—and most importantly—**the report represents you.** Neatness and promptness when delivery is required at a certain time also reflect on you. Be sure to leave the best possible impression on the people who read your written words.

IT TAKES PRACTICE

Placing a complete, well-written report on your boss's desk will give you a feeling of pride and accomplishment. Some supervisors may shy away from written words because they lack both confidence and know-how. Like any skill, memo and report writing requires plenty of practice and, if available, the coaching of an experienced person. If no such person is available, ask another supervisor to work with you. You can have fun while you learn from each other.

WHAT PRESENTATION TO USE

Printed Form Reports

Most companies have printed forms for reporting such subjects as personnel performance, employee ratings, suggestion system recommendations, quality inspection, customer complaints, accidents, grievances, absenteeism, and equipment maintenance. Filling out these reports is generally a matter of standard practice and procedure and is usually routine. These reports, however, are extremely important. They could be a prime factor in an arbitration, compensation case, claims adjustment, or personnel problem. When filling in a form report, always keep the end use in mind. Tell all the facts, but only those facts that you know are pertinent to the report. It is a good idea to check some of your recent reports with your boss or with the person who received them to be sure you are on the right track. Ask for suggestions or comments.

Memos

A memo (memorandum) is used primarily in interdepartmental communication. Whether on a printed company form or typed, it very often follows the style shown in Figure 9.

The body of a memo should deal briefly and directly with a single object. Normally, it is limited to the following questions: What are the facts? What do the facts mean? What ought to be done about the facts or situation?

Because of its simplicity, use the memo as a starting point to develop your mastery of report writing. Practice writing a memo to confirm a conversation with someone, or compose a memo in which you try to clear up a misunderstanding. Put some instructions or an explanation in memo form or report briefly on the progress of a certain project. Make the memo short. If possible, limit it to one page. A memo is for reporting, not documenting.

```
┌─────────────────────────────────────────────────────────────┐
│                                                               │
│                           MEMO                                │
│                                                               │
│    TO: _____  DATE:_____     │
│                                                               │
│    FROM:_____                    │
│                                                               │
│    SUBJECT:_____                   │
│                                                               │
│    _____  │
│                                                               │
│    _____  │
│                                                               │
│    _____  │
│                                                               │
└─────────────────────────────────────────────────────────────┘
```

Figure 9 A memo form, used primarily in interdepartmental communication.

Formal Reports

Formal reports vary widely in arrangement. You should check with your superior to see if your company prefers a given set-up or method of presentation. If there is no preference, the following outline may be used as a guide:

    I.   Title
   II.   Table of Contents (optional)
  III.   Introduction
  IV.   Summary of Conclusions and Recommendations
   V.   Body of the Report
  VI.   Appendix (when needed)

The *Title* should be placed in the center of the front page. Your name and date should be in the upper, right-hand corner. A short title that specifically describes the subject of the report commands immediate attention; take care to choose it well.

The *Table of Contents* is frequently used in lengthy reports. In brief reports, it can be omitted.

The *Introduction* covers background material explaining the purpose of the report. A typical beginning might be: "Recent quality control checks show that the rejection rate has risen 10 percent in Department K. Therefore, the purpose of this report is to. . . ."

The *Summary* is meant for the reader who may not take time to read your whole report but is interested in your recommendations. In the summary, you state your conclusions without elaborating on them. You may do this by summing up your ideas in a short paragraph, or you may separate your comments by enumerating the points in a column, as:

1. _____

2. _____

3. _____

In the summary, you are delivering your results, findngs, and/or recommendations. Take time to make them effective. The summary may be the most vital factor in getting your report across.

The *Body* of the report is where you present your substantiating information, facts, and data in detail. The body is the proper place for you to discuss your views and opinions. Everything must be presented in a logical order so that it all ties together in supporting your recommendations. Whenever possible, use known facts. However, if you are assuming something, do not fail to say so. Honesty and integrity are necessary or the reader will discount the whole report 'at the first unsubstantiated or inaccurate statement.

The *Appendix* may be necessary if you include any exhibits that you refer to in the report, such as previous reports, time studies, graphs, blueprints, calculations, or other statistical tables and compilations. Unless the report is of a technical nature, an appendix is usually not required.

HOW TO BEGIN

Select a quiet location where you can spread out your material on a table or desk. Before starting, get everything you will need.

Your report is actually started long before you sit down to write it. You may be preparing a report on your own initiative. If so, keep in mind the one purpose that is inspiring your action. Analyze what facts you have and those facts that you need to put over your viewpoint. Make your arrangement as airtight as possible.

On the other hand, you may be writing a report in response to a request from your supervisor. The procedure is the same. In addition, you must check and double-check to make certain that you have covered all the points requested and have anticipated questions that you may be asked about your statements.

No matter how well you have phrased your report, it is worthless if it does not convey your thoughts correctly or give the answers your boss requires.

The following ten steps can serve as a guide for getting started:

1. Understand thoroughly what you are to report on.
2. Ascertain all possible sources of information.
3. Decide what sources to draw on.
4. Gather the information.
5. Sift the information.
6. Review the information.
7. Keep what is useful and discard the rest.
8. Organize the information in logical order.
9. Summarize your findings.
10. Write the report.

HOW TO WRITE THE REPORT

Framing Thoughts

When you have organized the information in logical order and summarized your findings (Steps 8 and 9 in the Starting Guide above), you are ready to prepare an outline. Developing an outline is the ideal way of preparing to write because:

1. It is easier to move items in an outline from place to place than it is to rearrange the report after it has been written.
2. Outlining shows up gaps in the ideas or data.
3. The general theme will be clearer in your mind after preparing an outline.
4. The outline serves as a road map to keep you on the right road as you write.

Prepare the outline with the same care that you use to plan a trip. It is not a bothersome step; rather, it is the major tool in producing a report with a minimum of rewriting and a maximum of effect.

Words and Sentences

"The difference between the right word and almost the right word is the difference between lightning and the lightning bug," Mark Twain wrote. You may have heard a person about to write a report remark, "I know what to say, but I do not know how to say it." The answer is simple. Using your own words, say aloud exactly what comes to mind. Stop at the end of one thought and write down what you have said. Shortly, you will be writing directly on paper, using style and language with which you are comfortable and that sounds like you.

Two handy items to have for report writing are a good dictionary and a good grammar manual. Any good secretary's manual will contain sufficient grammar and punctuation aids. *Caution:* Do not fill the report with big words to impress your superiors. It is good to increase your vocabulary, but stick to words that are commonly used. Use punctuation accurately. You do not want your report to sound childishly simplistic, but avoid complex sentence structure unless it really serves some purpose.

Proofreading

When the rough copy of your report is finished, put it away and forget it for a day. This permits you to look anew from a fresh perspective when you are more likely to catch careless errors, faulty punctuation, poorly composed sentences, or omissions. Read the report over aloud. If you stumble over a sentence, phrase, or word, take a second look. Make corrections. Now let an associate, friend, or your spouse read the report. Listen to the criticisms and make changes that *you agree with.*

At this point, check the report for overall effect. See that it contains the "Seven C's of Good Report Writing": Clearness, Completeness, Conciseness, Correctness, Courtesy, Candor, Character.

Putting the Report Together

Your manuscript is now ready to be typed. If another person besides yourself is going to do the typing, be sure you have made the job as easy as possible. Review with the typist underlinings, spacings, identations, margins, number of copies needed, and general make-up. Remember, typists are paid to type, not to be clairvoyant! When the report has been typed and assembled, read it again yourself one last time. Present it to your superior with confidence.

EXTRA DIVIDENDS

The by-products of writing skill are almost as important as the skill itself. Developing skill in writing carries with it other improvements in one's ability. Let us examine some of the extra dividends.

Self-Discipline

Writing takes time and patience. Planning your time and sticking to your plan helps you to set personal goals and reach them.

Clear Thinking

The preparation that goes into a report includes sifting information. The ability to organize facts and weigh them stimulates the thought processes that lead to sound decisions. Making decisions is a vital part of the supervisory function.

Self-Confidence

When you have completed a well-written report, you will be as thoroughly informed on the subject as anyone in your organization. The knowledge gained by writing will lend self-assurance to your conversations with others.

Job Knowledge

Even though initial attempts at writing may not measure up to the standards you have set for yourself, it is important to realize that you will have learned a considerable amount about some aspect of your company. This alone repays you for the time spent.

Satisfaction

Your writing will form a bridge between yourself and others. Meetings of the mind thus accomplished will multiply your contacts and increase awareness of your presence in the company. Then your job will become more satisfying—a goal to be sought by all of us.

SKILL IN MEMO AND REPORT WRITING:
SKILL-BUILDING APPLICATION
HOW EFFECTIVELY DO I WRITE?

How many of the following questions can you answer *Yes?*

Clear

Are the words the simplest that could be used? _____

Do the words exactly express my thought? _____

Is the sentence structure clear? _____

Is each paragraph one complete thought unit? _____

Are all of the thoughts in proper order? _____

Complete

Does the report give all necessary information? _____

Does it answer all possible questions? _____

Concise

Does it contain only essential words and phrases? _____

Does it contain only essential facts? _____

Correct

Do the statements conform with company policy? _____

Are the facts accurate? _____

Are the grammar, spelling, and punctuation correct? _____

Courteous

Will the tone bring the desired response? _____

Is it free from antagonism? _____

Is it free from preaching and overbearing statements? _____

Candid

Have I been fair and honest? _____

Have I refrained from being overcritical of any person? _____

Have I given credit where credit is due? _____

Character

Is it neat in appearance and make-up? _____

Does it truly represent me? _____

Using this appraisal, judge each memo or report you write before you deliver it. Your answers will help you to discover in which areas your report writing needs improvement.

The "Seven C's of Good Report Writing" sum up the items you should consider when writing reports:

Clearness	Is the report understandable to a layman?
Completeness	Have *all* pertinent facts been given?
Conciseness	Is it to the point?
Correctness	Are the facts correct?
Courtesy	Am I fair to all people concerned?
Candor	Is it honest?
Character	Is it me?

Good writing takes self-discipline and practice. The skill of writing effective and useful reports and memos takes practice.

Memo Writing Application

The memo is a common form of written communications in industry. Write a brief memo to your supervisor explaining your recommendation(s) concerning safety meetings.

MEMO

TO:_____

DATE:_____

FROM:_____

SUBJECT:_____

_____

_____

_____

_____

_____

_____

_____

_____

CHECK YOUR MEMO USING THE REVIEW QUESTIONS ON THE PRECEDING PAGE.

REPORT WRITING APPLICATION

Another communication skill vital to all supervisors is being able to put down on paper vital facts that are important to the job.

Ask yourself: "Do I continue to postpone and avoid all writing? Am I self-conscious about my lack of writing ability? Do I avoid writing reports or details?" If you answered *yes* to any of these questions, this chapter on memo and report writing will help to develop the necessary skills needed so that you can talk on paper in an orderly, concise, and competent manner.

REPORT WRITING WORKSHEET

1. List the Topic/Title

    _____

2. Prepare an Outline

    _____

    _____

    _____

3. Introduce and State the Problem

    _____

    _____

    _____

    _____

4. Summary of Your Conclusions and Recommendations

    _____

    _____

    _____

    _____

    _____

    _____

5. Body of the Report

_____

_____

_____

_____

_____

_____

6. Complete Findings and Recommendations

_____

_____

_____

_____

_____

_____

IDEAS FOR IMPROVEMENT

From what you have learned in this chapter, list one or more specific actions that you intend to initiate within the next thirty days.

1. _____

   _____

   _____

   _____

   _____

   _____

2. _____

   _____

   _____

   _____

   _____

   _____

3. _____

   _____

   _____

   _____

   _____

   _____

REVIEW QUESTIONS

1. T   F   Memos are used primarily to communicate interdepartmental information.

2.   List the "Seven C's of Good Report Writing."

    _____

    _____

    _____

    _____

3.   Which of these "Seven C's" causes you the most problem?

4. T   F   No matter how well you have phrased a memo or report, it is worthless if it does not convey your thoughts correctly or give the answers the superior requires.

5.   What are some of the extra dividends or by-products of an improved writing skill?

    _____

    _____

    _____

CHAPTER 8

Skill in Reading Faster and Better

Keeping up on essential reading at work, as well as reading for pleasure, is not just a question of finding more time to read. The answer is to develop your reading skill.

This chapter will help you increase your reading speed and get more out of what you read. By practicing the techniques suggested here, you will be better equipped for supervision and will derive greater personal satisfaction from reading.

THE WRITTEN WORD

Your job success is more closely related to your ability to read faster and better than you may realize. No supervisor interested in improving her performance, getting more done, or in improving her effectiveness can afford to fall behind in her reading skill.

Job Demands

In every company, more information is being transmitted by the written word. With the volume of memos, bulletins, reports, specifications, pamphlets, trade magazines, and other written matter coming across your desk, you may feel that your entire work world is built on a mound of paper. The important things to know are how to read efficiently, how to save time, and how to keep up with essential job reading.

Thinking Power

Making decisions is the most important responsibility of any supervisor. Whether she succeeds or fails depends on her thinking ability. Her ability to think clearly, to grasp facts, and to absorb and understand ideas very often depends on how well she reads.

Out-thinking Competition

With plenty of business competition, every department supervisor needs to be concerned with cost control, efficiency, methods improvement, and understanding her work force. As a supervisor, you can profitably apply ideas, practical information, and the experience of other people and companies that you read about.

Profitable Pastime

To many supervisors, reading is sheer drudgery. Yet once reading skill is improved, it is no longer a chore. Even after working hours, you will look forward to reading material of your own choosing.

You can see why reading is considered such a vital skill by most supervisors. It is a practical skill. It is time-saving. Reading is essential for the progress of your career.

NEVER TOO LATE

It is never too late to start improving your reading ability. Regardless of education, many people read no better than they did in grade school and comprehend only 50 percent to 70 percent of what they read.

Fortunately, both speed and understanding can be readily increased. It is not unusual for a person to double reading ability. Reading is a skill you can master regardless of your age, educational level, or already crammed schedule. It does take interest, will power, and *practice*.

HOW TO PLAN YOUR READING

Basic Idea

To make your reading worthwhile, a lot depends on *what* you read and *how* you budget your time. You must read with a plan, not on a hit-or-miss basis. This means sizing up yourself in terms of your job, interests, living habits, and education. Plan your reading program to fit you.

Practice Pointers

Develop the habit of planning your reading by taking these steps:

1. Make a simple list of what you read, both on and off the job. Apply these questions to each item on your list.
    a. Of how much value is this to me?
    b. Am I spreading myself too thin?
    c. Is my reading always along the same line?
    d. Is this the best type of reading to help me on my job?
    e. Does this reading material make me a better-informed person?

You will probably get a new slant on your reading habits. You may read a newspaper but never pay much attention to the business section. Printed materials may come across your desk from which you benefit little, or you may overlook a wealth of reading material that is readily available.

2. Plan and budget your reading time. You probably have more time available for reading than you realize.
    a. Be careful about selecting what you read and you will get better results in less time.
    b. Try setting aside a certain time each day for reading. You may be able to budget your working hours to provide some specific time each day for reading routine paper work and other miscellaneous material. Reading the last half hour before bed may be an ideal way to relax. You may have an extra ten minutes after lunch to browse through a magazine on industrial or business practices.

c. Have you ever tried reading with specific goals in mind? Some supervisors read with the purpose of picking up one new practical idea a day, or of reading half a dozen books a year.

HOW TO CONCENTRATE WHEN YOU READ

Basic Idea

Reading is more than looking at words; it is getting the meaning out of those words. This requires that you free your mind of distractions and keep your thoughts from wandering. A good reader's mind is always intent on understanding.

Practice Pointers

You can learn to concentrate on your reading by practicing these pointers:

1. If your mind is easily distracted, try finding a quiet spot where you can read, or leave your heavy, detailed reading for a time when you are alone.
2. Before you start reading, fix some specific questions in your mind that you want answered. Jot these questions down. Look for specific ideas that may apply to your job.
3. As you read, argue mentally with the writer, just as if the two of you were actually talking. Think in terms of, "Does this sound right?" Or, "Is this what my experience shows?"
4. Take an interest in word mastery by using the dictionary. Look up words that you do not know in order to increase your reading vocabulary.

HOW TO SKIM

Basic Idea

Skimming is like taking the cream off the top of the milk. It is a skill that helps you to pick up the main ideas. Skimming will increase your reading speed considerably, but it must be used properly. *It never pays to sacrifice understanding for speed.*

Practice Pointers

When and how to skim:

1. Before thoroughly reading an article, report, or book, quickly scan the headlines, paragraph headings, title pages, or bold-face type. You can skip over details as long as you pull together the main thoughts. This method can be used to help you determine whether you ought to go back and read in more detail. If you decide to read in detail, you will find that what you read will be more organized and meaningful.
2. Concentrate on the first and last sentence of a paragraph. These lines often summarize the subject matter of the entire paragraph.
3. When you are looking up references or answers to a problem, let your eyes quickly travel over the written material. The specific information you seek will tend to pop out at you.

HOW TO AVOID BAD READING HABITS

Basic Idea

Reading for both speed and understanding means that you must develop the right reading habits. Fortunately, most poor reading habits can be overcome.

Practice Pointers

How many of these reading habits do you have?

1. If you form words with your lips and tongue as you read, you are holding yourself back. Your eyes can easily take in words two to three times faster than you can say them. Concentrate on *seeing* the words. Force yourself not to say the words or to move your lips. (Suggestion: Hold your tongue lightly between your teeth.)
2. Most poor readers read word-by-word and re-read words that they miss. A good reader will try to make only three or four pauses per line. (Suggestion: When you watch television, try to read all of the credits that flash on the screen at one time.)
3. Many people do not read fast for fear they will miss something.

Very often, however, by trying to read faster you actually comprehend more of what you read. Try forcing yourself to read a little faster and make your eyes sweep across the page.

4. Finally, do not move your head from side to side, and do not follow across the line with your finger or with a pencil.

HOW TO REMEMBER WHAT YOU READ

Basic Idea

Skill in reading pays off only if you remember what you have read. For any supervisor, time spent reading is too valuable to be wasted. It must result in either greater knowledge, better understanding, or in practical application to your job.

Practice Pointers

You can remember more of what you read if you practice these steps:

1. After reading several paragraphs or a section, pause for a moment and summarize the main points in your own words.
2. Try talking to other people about what you have read. The act of explaining to another person what you have read will help you to retain the thoughts longer.
3. Do you use a reading file? It is simple to start one. Take a folder and regularly drop reading notes into it, or even copies of whole articles. (*Caution:* Put away only those items you really plan to use. Otherwise you will be collecting useless paper.)

PRACTICING FOR RESULTS

It takes plenty of practice to make your reading pay off. Here are some suggestions:

Set A Goal

As soon as you have finished this chapter, resolve to improve your reading skill. If you are not a good reader, you can become one. Rather than waiting until tomorrow, start with the *very next thing* you read.

Pace Yourself

Start off by taking an article, memo, or report and estimate the number of words. Then, by keeping in mind the basic skills in this chapter, time yourself on how long it takes you to finish. See for yourself how much you really comprehend. By checking your speed and comprehension regularly, you will quickly see results.

Outside Help

You can get additional help to supplement your reading self-improvement program. Many communities offer adult education reading courses. Some companies provide training courses in reading improvement for their employees. There are also a number of good commercial reading-improvement courses in all price ranges. Bear in mind, however, that no course or program in the world (including this one) will be of any value to you if *you* do not follow through with discipline and the desire for improvement.

SKILL IN READING FASTER AND BETTER: SKILL-BUILDING APPLICATION

Continuing your communication skills, you are now looking at keeping up to date on essential reading relative to work. Good reading habits are not just a question of finding more time, rather they involve learning to develop our reading speed and skill. Many of us have literally quit reading anything other than the local newspaper.

This chapter contains several ideas on how to concentrate better when reading and some techniques in skimming that will increase reading speed. We also examined some bad reading habits and offered some corrective points for each.

Again, the real skill in reading starts when you begin to read more and to plan more for important reading.

ASSIGNMENT: Choose a book on self-development or some pertinent business subject. After reading the book, discuss it briefly with a friend, spouse, fellow employee, or your supervisor.

READING TIPS

1. Plan and budget your reading time.
2. Try to concentrate on the real meaning of what you are reading.
3. Practice skimming.
4. Make note of any bad habits that are creeping back into your reading.
5. Practice on the suggestions contained in the section, "Remembering More About What You Are Reading."

Selective Reading is important in avoiding obsolescence in your job!

IDEAS FOR IMPROVEMENT

From what you have learned in this chapter, list one or more specific actions that you intend to initiate within the next thirty days.

1. _____

   _____

   _____

   _____

   _____

   _____

2. _____

   _____

   _____

   _____

   _____

   _____

3. _____

   _____

   _____

   _____

   _____

   _____

REVIEW QUESTIONS

	Most of time	Occasion- ally	Seldom
1. Do I read for pleasure? (Other than newspaper)	_____	_____	_____
2. Do I read at least one business journal a month?	_____	_____	_____
3. Do I read what the competi- tion—our competitors— are doing?	_____	_____	_____
4. Am I aware of trends and happenings within my industry?	_____	_____	_____

5. List a book you have read in the last thirty days. (Any topic)

   _____

6. Define *skimming.* _____

   _____

7. What are at least two of the bad reading habits listed that you need to overcome?

   _____

   _____

8. T   F   In reading, you should never sacrifice understanding for speed.

9. T   F   If you are easily distracted, it is best to find a relatively quiet spot to read.

10.   Complete the reading assignment listed earlier on read- ing a book on self-development and discussing it with a friend. Continue to practice the reading tips discussed.

CHAPTER 9

Skill in Selling Your Ideas

I t is not enough to have good ideas—their merits also must be presented convincingly. More supervisors and managers fail from lack of skill in selling their ideas than from lack of having ideas. This chapter will apply the best techniques of salesmanship to the selling of ideas on the job.

SUPERVISION IS SALESMANSHIP

Salesmanship has been defined as the capacity to get people to act, the ability to persuade others to support an idea willingly. What better definition is there of supervision?

In its broadest meaning, salesmanship is required in almost every supervisory activity. When you, as a supervisor, must introduce a new rule or policy to your workers, you are *selling*. When you recommend a new procedure or piece of office equipment to your supervisor, you must *sell* your superior on it. If you are a staff specialist, you must constantly *sell* your ideas and services. If you convince another department head on how to solve a joint problem, you are also using salesmanship.

WHY "NO SALE"?

The basic objective of most face-to-face communication on the job is to *sell an idea*. A person needs to understand a communication in order to give his best support to it. He needs to accept an idea before he will do more than just go through the motions.

You have what seems to be a first-rate idea. It looks like a natural. But when it is presented, it falls flat. Rejected. "No sale."

What happened? Many things can go wrong, of course. Here are some of the most common reasons that ideas are rejected:

> The idea itself is faulty. It may be based on unsound assumptions or incomplete facts.
>
> Overselling. In your enthusiasm to present an idea favorably, you may have understated the drawbacks or overstated the advantages of the idea.
>
> Lack of concrete proposal. The person on the receiving end of your idea wants to know exactly what you recommend, not just an explanation of everything that is wrong with present practices.
>
> Resistance to change. Basic human reluctance to try something new accounts for many idea rejections. Then, too, some people unconsciously react negatively to new ideas unless they have had some hand in shaping the plans.

If an idea is rejected, you must re-examine your techniques of selling. If the buyer has not bought, then the seller has not sold.

In the next section, we will consider the six basic steps of selling as they apply to putting ideas across on the job. By study and drill, you can learn to sell.

Step 1.   Know Your Product

Selling Problem

Supervisor Rob Terry knew that a new piece of equipment would increase output. So he presented his recommendations to his superior: "Looks like it makes sense, Rob. What does it cost?"

Rob realized too late that he was not armed with all the facts he needed. All he could say was, "I do not know; I will have to check."

Practice Pointers

Be thoroughly familiar with facts and figures. In selling an idea, think through your idea and have all the facts at hand. To be sure that you are on firm ground, ask yourself these questions:

1. Does the idea meet a definite, present need?
2. Exactly what is the idea I plan to present? As a check, try writing out a brief, clear statement of the proposal.
3. Does the idea include specific action steps? Does it answer the question, "How can it be done?"
4. What will the proposal cost in workers, materials, money, and time?
5. Of what value is the idea to the company? Why should dollars be invested in this scheme rather than in some other profitable way?
6. What assumptions have I made in developing my proposal? Assumptions should be noted and, where possible, verified.
7. What advantages and benefits can be expected? What disadvantages or objections may develop?
8. What alternatives are there for reaching the same objectives?
9. What part should I play in presenting the idea? Should the proposal be turned over to someone else? Should other people be included?
10. With whom can I discuss the idea to test its soundness? Often an informal discussion with other supervisors will indicate a need for additional facts or investigation.

Before you try to convince anyone else, make sure that you are convinced; and if you cannot convince yourself, drop the subject. Do not try to put over anything. If your idea stands up under your own critical questioning, you should be ready for the next step in planning your sales presentation.

Step II.   Know Your Prospect

Selling Problem

Supervisor Larry Short worked out the details of a plan to change the time-card procedures in his department. He knew that he would first have to get his superior's okay, and then he would have the task of selling his people on the change. He reasoned correctly that he would have to use different approaches. His superior would be interested in his analysis of clerical costs and in the attendance control problem. On the other hand, the employees might be persuaded by the personal convenience angle.

Practice Pointers

Larry was applying an important rule of good salesmanship—know your prospect. The better you know the person or group you are trying to sell, the better the chances of putting your ideas across. In analyzing your prospect:

1. Be sure you have found the right person to sell to.
2. Try to put yourself in the buyer's shoes. Analyze how you would react to the idea if you were an employee, the superior, or another supervisor, depending on who your prospect is.
3. Identify the buyer's viewpoint, attitudes, and desires. How has the buyer reacted to similar ideas in the past? Plan to associate the new idea with ideas already supported and accepted by the buyer's plans and goals.
4. Anticipate questions and objections. Be ready with the answers.

Step III.   Plan the Approach

Selling Problem

Supervisor Bob Johnson rushed into the office manager's office. He figured he had the answer to a problem they had both talked about. He presented his idea carefully and completely. Yet, his superior seemed impatient and showed little interest. Bob did not know that his superior was trying to finish up a report requested by the division head. Where did Bob miss the boat?

Practice Pointers

Most sales people recognize the importance of planning the approach to the customer. In planning your approach, answer four specific questions about the sales presentation: When? Where? How? Who?

When involves the problem of timing:

1. Select an opportunity when your prospect has ample time to listen.

2. Guard against interruptions.
3. Consider whether it is best to present your idea in small doses or all at one time.
4. An excellent time, of course, is when your idea applies to a current problem.

Where includes choosing the setting. This, too, may influence the person on the receiving end of your proposal. Should you meet with this prospect alone or should other people be included? Should you meet in an office? Whose? A conference room? Where? Over lunch?

How means backing up your presentation. The sales person in the field makes effective use of aids and point-of-sale displays. Your presentation, too, may benefit from the use of diagrams, charts, blackboard notes, or a preliminary written report.

Who refers to whether or not this person can buy? This question is so essential, it should probably be asked first instead of last. Good sales people qualify their buyers ahead of time to see that they are the people with the checkbook. Does the person to whom you propose selling your idea have the *authority* or *decision-making power* to put your idea into operation? If the answer is "no," you might want to reconsider and pick a more likely buyer.

Step IV. Present Your Idea

Selling Problem

A supplier's salesperson left the office of Ron Warren. Later, Ron thought to himself, "Nice person. Seems to know everything about the supplies. Yet, she has never shown me how I can save any money with her line of supplies." How had the salesperson failed in making her sales presentation?

Practice Pointers

The outline for any sales presentation states a case and then proves it. Here is how you can present your idea concisely and persuasively:

1. State your idea as simply and clearly as possible.
2. Present the idea's benefits and features.
   a. A *benefit* answers the prospect's question, "What will this idea do for me, my department, or the company?"
   b. A *feature* explains how or why.

Here we have the crux of successful selling. The supply salesperson was able to present many product *features*. She failed because she did not present clear-cut *benefits*. She did not answer Ron's question, "What will this do for my department?"

When a *benefit* is supported by a *feature*, it becomes a doubly powerful selling tool.

> General Form: This idea will accomplish for you (*benefit*) because this is so (*feature*).
>
> Specific Example: This plan will reduce your material handling costs (*benefit*) by replacing manual methods with an automatic conveyor (*feature*).

Practice developing selling points in which idea benefits are supported by unique features.

3. Conclude by restating your idea and its advantages. Be enthusiastic without overselling. Be confident.

If you try to sell what is best for you, you are likely to fail. But if you sell what is best for the buyer, you are more likely to make the sale, and then both of you benefit.

Step V.   Handle Objections

Selling Problem

Employees in Roger Fleer's department began to raise some questions about a new policy he had just described to them. Some of their comments caught Roger off guard. By the time the meeting was over, he was on the defensive. What started off as a selling job ended in Roger's delivering ultimatums. Both he and the policy had lost face in the eyes of the workers.

Practice Pointers

Through experience, a sales person learns to expect and to handle customer objections. The following three suggestions will help you handle objections successfully.

1. Be a good listener. You have had your say. Now let the prospect ask the questions. Be alert to the unasked question that may lie behind a verbal comment.

2. Anticipate objections. Have facts and answers ready. Present additional benefits and features.
3. Above all, avoid arguments. Deal with objections calmly and patiently. If you have marshalled your facts, you should have no difficulty in overcoming sales resistance.

Step VI.   Close the Sale

Selling Problem

Terry Dunn had mapped out his plans for a new accident-prevention campaign. His superior had listened with interest and asked some questions about the cost of posters he proposed having made. Then, sensing that his superior might want some time to think over the ideas Terry suggested, he said, "Why not sleep on it? We can start the program any time you are ready. Let me know if you need any other information."

Practice Pointers

The seller is eager to *close the sale* to get the buyer to say, "I will take it." As an idea seller, you may be anxious for acceptance. Yet, it is often unwise to press for too quick a decision. Most people do not want to feel that an idea is being jammed down their throat. In some cases, the prospect may have to consult other people. On the other hand, if the situation seems favorable, go for an immediate decision. In closing the sale:

1. Encourage a sense of partnership for the final outcome—share credit for the idea.
2. If a favorable decision is reached, try to pin down action points and details. When action is to be taken, find out: Who will be responsible, what follow-up steps are necessary, and who should be informed.
3. If a decision is postponed, follow up after a reasonable time.
4. Do not be discouraged if your idea is finally turned down. If you have followed through with each step of your sales presentation, you will gain respect for being thorough and businesslike.

THOUGHTS FOR IDEA SELLERS

When trying to sell an idea, consider these five thoughts:

1. My superiors may see my idea differently. They have had to judge many ideas such as mine. Sometimes they have backed the wrong idea and have been in trouble for it.
2. My ideas are new, and, therefore, may seem dangerous.
3. I must, therefore, show clearly not only the advantage of my idea, but also why it is reasonable to expect success.
4. I must be considerate. I will not criticize the old way. But I will make crystal clear the merits of the new and give credit where it is due.
5. My idea benefits my organization as well as myself.

SKILL IN SELLING YOUR IDEAS:
SKILL-BUILDING APPLICATION
KNOW THE BENEFITS AND FEATURES

List at least three benefits of your ideas. (A benefit answers the question, "What will the idea do for me, my department, my company?")

1. _____
   _____
   _____
   _____

2. _____
   _____
   _____
   _____

3. _____
   _____
   _____

List the Ideas' Feature(s). (A feature explains how or why.)

1. _____
   _____
   _____
   _____

2. _____
   _____
   _____
   _____

APPLICATION

How many times have you gone home upset, angry, or frustrated because a good idea that you had was turned down, not accepted as you knew it should be, or was not even given the time of day?!

It has been stated that salesmanship is the capacity or ability to persuade other persons to support your ideas willingly and happily. Let us examine and apply some of the best techniques of modern salesmanshp to the selling of ideas on our job.

ASSIGNMENT: Identify a problem, suggestion, or recommendation you feel your company ought to examine, put into being, or adopt. Prepare and present this idea to your supervisor.

SELLING YOUR IDEA
WORKSHEET

(Listed are the six steps in selling an idea. Write in the appropriate information about each step.)

1. Know the Product   (Be thoroughly familiar with the strengths, weaknesses, costs, and time necessary.)

   _____

   _____

   _____

   _____

   _____

2. Know your Prospect   (Put yourself in your prospect's shoes. Anticipate your selling problems.)

   _____

   _____

   _____

   _____

   _____

3. Plan your Approach   (When, Where, How, Who)

When _____

_____

_____

Where _____

_____

_____

How _____

_____

_____

_____

_____

Who _____

_____

_____

4. Present your Idea

Idea's Benefit _____

_____

_____

_____

Idea's Feature _____

_____

_____

_____

_____

5. Handle Objections   (Have possible answers ready.)

_____

_____

_____

_____

6. Close the Sale   (Now or later?)
    Do you logically expect an on-the-spot decision?

    _____

    What follow-up do you anticipate? _____

    _____

    _____

    _____

    _____

IDEAS FOR IMPROVEMENT

From what you have learned in this chapter, list one or more specific actions that you intend to initiate within the next thirty days.

1. _____
   _____
   _____
   _____
   _____
   _____
   _____

2. _____
   _____
   _____
   _____
   _____
   _____

3. _____
   _____
   _____
   _____
   _____
   _____
   _____

REVIEW QUESTIONS

1.   The definition for salesmanship is also an excellent definition for supervision. Write that definition.

_____

_____

_____

2.   T   F   More supervisors and managers fail from lack of skill in selling their ideas than from lack of having ideas.

3.   T   F   People must be able to understand and communicate ideas in order to give them their best support.

4.   Several common reasons that ideas are rejected were studied. List the two most important reasons from your viewpoint.

_____

_____

_____

_____

5.   T   F   There is no need or place for salesmanship skills in a supervisory job.

6.   What question does an idea's *benefit* answer?

_____

_____

_____

7.   What question does an idea's *feature* explain or answer?

_____

_____

_____

8.   T   F   It is extremely important to anticipate objections and have facts and answers ready.

9.   What was the main point you got out of the section "Closing the Sale"?

_____

_____

_____

10.   Complete and review the assignment in the application section by presenting an idea to your superior that you feel your company should adopt.

CHAPTER 10

Skill in Evaluating People

E very day, a supervisor must reach decisions based on his or her evaluation of people; he or she must make decisions sizing up a job applicant, in recommending a person for promotion, in analyzing and correcting performance problems. The principles of employee rating can be learned. The skills of appraising people can be self-taught.

DIFFERENCES MAKES
THE DIFFERENCE

What a different world it would be if people were not so different! And, it might be added, how uninteresting!

An incontestable fact that every supervisor faces daily is that each person he contacts is a unique individual with a distinct personality. Every person begins with inborn traits and aptitudes. You are shaped by all that goes on around you and by all that you experience. You are driven by learned behaviors that condition your behavior—your desire for recognition, family interests, competitive instincts, your pride in accomplishment, and your drive for self-preservation.

All of these human forces help to mold and to make each person distinctly different. It is these differences that present a daily challenge to supervisory understanding.

TWO TYPICAL TASKS

Because of human differences, a supervisor must make evaluations and arrive at decisions about people. At one time or another, you probably will become involved in two typical tasks:

1. Sizing up or appraising candidates for employment, upgrading, demotion, or transfer.
2. Rating or appraising employee performance for the purpose of setting earning levels, planning needed training, or correcting performance problems.

Fortunately, to reach sound decisions and to improve your appraisal evaluations you need not be a trained psychologist. There are bench marks—*job specifications* and *standards of performance*—on which to base your appraisals. Interviewing skills and employee rating skills can be used to sharpen your judgment.

AN ESSENTIAL SKILL

When dealing with workers as individuals, a competent supervisor can learn to show them exactly how their work can best be done; to guide, help, and encourage them; and, at the same time, to study their possibilities as workers.

Since supervisors and managers must get their results through people, no managerial skill is more essential than that of evaluating people intelligently and competently. The wrong person on a key task can counteract your best efforts and can adversely affect the good work of others. To be able to recognize ability, apptitude, and intelligence in other people is equally important to the supervisor's success as is the possession of these same qualities.

I: HOW TO SIZE UP JOB CANDIDATES

Avoid the pitfall of thinking that you can size up candidates accurately by a brief survey of their appearance or after a few minutes of conversation. Candidates for employment, promotion, or transfer must all be carefully screened and appraised. To select the right person and reach sound placement decisions, the supervisor should master the following basic skills.

Skill In Determining Job Requirements

Supervisor Joe Leonard was on the spot. Three times in as many months he had chosen replacements for the keypunch job in payroll. One employee had been just plain lazy. Another had been energetic, but so inaccurate that all of the work had to be redone. And now, the third employee had quit feeling that the job was tedious and boring.

In desperation, Joe asked himself, "What kind of person does this job really call for? What sort of employee should I be looking for?"

What Joe Leonard needed, and what you need when there is a job to fill, is a set of job specifications—a detailed list of requirements that defines the right person for the job.

Skill Suggestion

Draw up a set of job specifications for one or two key jobs under your supervision. Use the following check list to be sure that you have not overlooked any important requirements of the job.

JOB SPECIFICATION CHECK LIST

(Note any critical requirements of the job. Be specific.)

1.	Education:	Consider the minimum schooling required.
2.	Special schooling:	Note any additional trade school or course requirements.

3. Work experience: Consider amount and nature of essential previous work experience.

4. Special skills: Record any necessary abilities or skills.

5. Ability to learn: Consider intelligence necessary to master new information or acquire additional skills.

6. Physical demands: Review all physical activities and requirements.

7. Working conditions: Note specific conditions and safety factors.

8. Contact with others: Consider relations the employee will have to maintain within and outside organization.

9. Responsibility for company property: Consider degree of reliability demanded.

10. Leadership: Consider extent to which employee must direct work of others.

11. Potential: Consider normal promotional pattern and what additional requirements this may impose.

12. Other requirements: Review any other special requirements for the job, including evaluation and initiative necessary.

Skill in Interviewing

Do candidate qualifications match job specifications? This is the basic question you must answer during the selection interview. In addition, you will want to know if the candidate is someone you can work with and who will fit into your group. Does the candidate have the ability to learn? Does the candidate have the interest and capacity to move up to other jobs?

Skill Guide

Here are ten practical points for the supervisor who wishes to sharpen up interviewing skills.

1. Prepare for the interview by reviewing the specifications of the job to be filled. Organize a simple, straightforward interview plan by jotting down the key questions you want to ask.

2. Provide for privacy during the interview.

3. Put the candidate at ease. Be friendly, courteous, calm. Begin with simple, factual questions.

4. Do not be swayed by initial appearances or first impressions. You may have heard someone say, "I go on vibes; I know the right person as soon as he or she walks through the door." He is usually wrong.

5. Recognize your own biases. You may be influenced by past experiences with persons who remind you of the candidate. Judge on the basis of facts.

6. Do not play amateur psychologist. A job interview is no place for character analysis. Your aim is to determine the facts concerning the candidate's qualifications.

7. Give the candidate an opportunity to speak freely and to ask questions. The interview should be informative to the prospect. This person, after all, will be deciding whether he or she wants to work for you, too.

8. Make use of simple tests of working knowledge or skill.

9. Seek the evaluation of other people. Your superior or another supervisor may pick up helpful facts and impressions during additional interviews.

10. Conclude the interview by reaching a decision or by indicating when the candidate can expect a decision. End on a friendly note. Follow up.

II: HOW TO MEASURE EVALUATION OF EMPLOYEE PERFORMANCE

Whether your company has a regular employee-rating procedure or has supervisors develop their own informal systems, here are the basic skills required for appraising work results.

Skill in Setting
Performance Standards

To measure employees' performance and gauge their progress, you must know what their job duties are. You must also have some bench marks or standards of performance that describe how much they should do and how well.

Practice Drill

Try developing some precise written statements of work standards. These standards should define minimum, acceptable levels of job performance, such as:

Produces part *A* at an average rate of 50 or more units per hour and with an inspection-acceptance average of 95 percent or better.

Maintains his workplace in orderly condition with an average housekeeping rating of 80 or better.

Types 60 words per minute with 95 percent accuracy.

In each statement of a performance standard, include some measurable factor. This factor will permit later measurement of above and below standard performance.

Skill in Gathering
Performance Data

Successful employee rating plans demand periodic and systematic review of performance. Most supervisors, however, find it difficult to rely on their own general impressions of an employee's work over a period of time. Instead, they keep whatever individual records are necessary to measure performance in relation to key job standards.

It is one thing to rate an employee as excellent, good, fair, or poor. It is more important to be able to support such evaluations with evidence of actual accomplishment or lack of accomplishment on the job.

Practice Technique

On a "Critical Performance Record" note actual incidents that affect job success or failure.

Skill in Rating People

When used with understanding, a rating scale helps a supervisor to focus attention on relevant traits and to record evaluations with greater accuracy and consistency than is otherwise possible.

When is a rating a sound rating? When it is based on a thoughtful review of actual work results and when the rater has put aside personal feelings and prejudiced evaluations. Supervisors can remove guesswork from employee rating and appraisal by basing their people-evaluation on facts, standards, qualifications, and results.

Pitfalls and Pointers

Every rater must guard against some very common pitfalls. By making a conscious effort to avoid them, supervisors can become skilled evaluators of people.

Pitfalls: Common Problems in Rating	Pointers: Suggested Safeguards
1. *The Halo Effect:* The common tendency of raters to allow a single factor, such as an employee's cooperativeness, to overbalance the evaluating of other factors, such as quality, productivity, and housekeeping.	Consider each aspect or factor of employee performance separately. Try to relate each factor to performance facts. Be ready to support ratings with evidence.
2. *Personal bias:* Letting personal feelings, likes, or dislikes color the appraisal. ("I do not like the way he parts his hair.")	Try to be fair. Do not let friendships, off-the-job relationships, or prejudice affect the ratings. Avoid overrating people you have hired and trained yourself, and vice versa.
3. *Clustering:* Rating all employees uniformly high or low; being too tough or too easy with everyone.	Discuss your rating standards with other people. Review ratings with your superior to sharpen your evaluations of

performance distinctions. Normally, expect a few employees to rate high, a few low, and more distributed in the middle range. Experiment by ranking employees in the order of their proficiency.

4. *Average tendency:* Rating an employee as an average in every respect. Taking the easy way out to avoid being committed.

Face the facts and call the shots as you see them. Each employee tends to be outgoing (either good or poor) in some respects.

5. *Job influence:* Rating the importance of the job instead of the performance of the person doing the job.

Try not to be influenced by the value of the job or the qualifications needed to do it. Concentrate on the results the person on the job is getting.

6. *Age, sex, and service bias:* Being influenced by the age, sex, service, earnings level, or previous experience of the person being rated.

Again, the rater should only be concerned with how well the employee is performing in relation to work standards.

7. *The isolated case:* Basing performance ratings on nontypical, isolated incidents.

Refer to your "Critical Performance Record" to see whether incidents are unusual or typical. Base appraisals on normal, everyday work.

SKILL IN EVALUATING PEOPLE:
SKILL-BUILDING APPLICATION

Are you wasting the talent of the people working for you? You may be, if you are not a good evaluator of people, or are not showing concern for their performance and communicating this to them.

The supervisor who knows the strengths and weaknesses of subordinates is in a better position to make sound decisions regarding their potential, development, work assignments, and rewards.

If you think of the best manager you have ever worked for in business or industry, usually one key attribute and skill that person possessed was probably the ability to size up individuals. By using the exercises in this chapter as a model, you can improve your ability to evaluate people in the workplace.

ASSIGNMENT: To develop skills in evaluating people, you first need to practice evaluating yourself. Complete the "Critical Performance Record" on yourself for the past ninety days by listing two or three favorable and unfavorable incidents/events.

Critical Performance Record [sample]			
Name John Jones			
Favorable Incidents		Unfavorable Incidents	
Date	What Happened?	Date	What Happened?
2/20	Completed a rush job for key customer	3/26	Had an argument with Nancy about doing a rush job
4/27	Handled an irate customer very well	5/1	Left early without permission
5/19	Got an extension on the special report deadline		

CRITICAL PERFORMANCE
WORKSHEET

Name_____

Time Period _____

FAVORABLE INCIDENTS		UNFAVORABLE INCIDENTS	
Date	What Happened?	Date	What Happened?

Copy this form and maintain a critical performance worksheet on each of your employees.

IDEAS FOR IMPROVEMENT

From what you have learned in this chapter, list one or more specific actions that you intend to initiate within the next thirty days.

1. _____
   _____
   _____
   _____
   _____
   _____
   _____

2. _____
   _____
   _____
   _____
   _____
   _____
   _____

3. _____
   _____
   _____
   _____
   _____
   _____
   _____

REVIEW QUESTIONS

1. T   F   All human beings are created differently, which presents to the manager the most challenging aspect of understanding people.

2. T   F   Because the supervisor must get results through people, no managerial skill is more essential than that of evaluating people intelligently and completely.

3. T   F   You therefore must become a trained psychologist in order to be a good supervisor.

4. T   F   In learning to size up people, the most important task is first to learn to size up yourself.

5.   In looking at your own job, a very important ingredient is a set of job specifications. Write in your definition of your key job specifications.

_____

_____

_____

_____

6.   In placing the "right person in the right job," you are really examining the person's _____ versus the job specifications.

7.   You learned how to set performance standards on your job. As a practice exercise, list two well-defined minimum acceptance levels of job performance that you feel are important on your job.

_____

_____

_____

_____

8.   In this chapter, we learned what a *written work standard* is. Define this term.

_____

_____

9.   In evaluating people, several common pitfalls in rating were discussed. List the one pitfall that you feel causes you the most difficulty in rating. Why does it?

_____

_____

_____

10.   Complete the worksheet on a "Critical Performance Record" of your past ninety days. Follow the format for your employees.

CHAPTER 11

Skill in Exercising Authority

A uthority does not come from any single source. It comes from the capacity, understanding, judgment, and imagination shown by the person in authority.

Throughout the business world, management personnel are vested with the responsibility for leading profitable operations. To carry out this responsibility effectively, managers have authority over the people and functions they supervise.

The purpose in this book is to clarify the nature of authority and to suggest specific ways in which you as a supervisor can sharpen your ability to exercise authority.

DOUBLE ROLE—AN OBSTACLE
OR A BRIDGE?

No matter what position in management you hold, (see chapter one, Figure 1) you find yourself in two positions relative to authority:

1. As a *leader of people,* you have a certain range of authority.
2. As a *subordinate to others,* you work under the authority of one or more persons.

The two relationships may seem completely opposite—one as a leader, one as subordinate—and yet, they are closely tied. The atmosphere of authority created by the person and organization above inevitably affects the atmosphere of authority the supervisor creates below.

If you are a new supervisor, the chances are that you came up through the ranks of your company, showing the powers that be that you are technically competent and capable where the work and activities of your department are concerned. It is also likely, however, that some of the people you now supervise consider you to be their friend. Because you probably wish to maintain some of these friendships, it is especially important that you consider how you exercise your authority.

A manager cannot hope to—nor should she want to—insulate herself from authority above. Rather, she must accept and interpret orders from above in a way that will be most effective in carrying them out with the employees below. As a supervisor, you must identify yourself as being part of the management. Some managers feel that authority evolves from positions on an organization chart, but real authority evolves from competence; and competence in turn, from tested experience.

You will want to apply what you learn in this chapter to your position both as leader and subordinate.

CONFUSION ABOUT AUTHORITY

To supervisors, *authority* is a well-known term. Yet some confusion has resulted about its real meaning. These points should clarify the nature of authority.

Authority Means Discipline. Too often, exercising authority is thought of as using discipline or not using discipline. Certainly, there is much more to authority. Whenever a supervisor takes action with subordinates, directly or indirectly, authority is being exercised.

Responsibility Requires Authority. It is true that a supervisor should have sufficient authority to carry out the functions over which she has been given responsibility. But the problem is not as simple as it sounds. Frequently, a supervisor shares authority with other people who do not share the responsibility. The supervisor must learn to live within a complex structure of authority shared between herself, staff people, her superiors, and occasionally her subordinates.

Team Effort Rather Than Authority. A team without a coach rarely wins games. Similarly, authority exists in the business organization because of a group's basic need for leadership and direction. Effective teamwork results from sound use of authority. Conversely, good team effort rarely occurs without the proper exercise of authority.

PRINCIPLES OF EXERCISING AUTHORITY

Wouldn't you like the kind of operation in which everybody did his or her job well? Where tensions and arguments did not exist? Where costs were low, service to customers perfect? Where things always ran smoothly? The extent to which these ideals could exist depends greatly on how authority is exercised. People often submit willingly, even cheerfully, to authority when they believe it to be exercised well and responsibly in the pursuit of ends of which they approve and in whose benefits they will share.

The following Principles of Authority govern the degree of success of an organization. Also given are Practice Situations and Check Points designed to help you gain practical experience in improving your skill in exercising authority.

Principle I: Authority is Conferred from Above but Earned from Below

If you are to be wise in the use of your aurhority, you will always guard the self-respect of the people under you. You will create an atmosphere in which others can develop a feeling of significant participation and a measure of self-determination. Authority that is of lasting influence depends on personal integrity and competency.

Authority to lead is earned from subordinates, through gaining mutual respect and confidence. This is true regardless of the fact that the organization chart specifies an individual's authority over subordinates.

Practice Situation	*Check Points*
Employees reporting to supervisor Sue Thomas always go to her superior on impor-	Sue Thomas must determine why employees do not honor her authority.

tant matters. Sue exerts little influence over their actions on critical problems. She has authority on paper but has not earned the necessary confidence of employees to have real authority.

It is because of distrust fear of extreme action, or hesitation?

A supervisor in this position cannot carry out her responsibilities for costs, quality, and efficiency.

Undoubtedly, to earn authority, she must take action both below and above her.

Principle II: The Primary Goal of Authority is Job-Centered Assistance

Service to people below and above in order to help them perform their jobs better is one of the most overlooked aspects of authority. Authority implies control and power, yet these result only when employees are performing their jobs satisfactorily and when superiors' use of authority is largely in harmony with the supervisor's.

Practice Situation
Supervisor Jim Matthewson constantly instructed his workers in their job techniques. He emphasized fundamentals, not frills. He talked results and inspired attitudes. Employees frequently came to him with questions and ideas. He was willing to help. Generally, his people performed well.

Check Points
People who are helped need less direction and become more competent.

Job-centered activity builds good attitudes without the need for soul-searching discussions.

Creative improvements come from mutual assitance of supervisor and subordinates.

Principle III: Important Advantages Result When Authority Is Passed Down the Line

Authority should be exercised so that as much authority as possible is delegated to subordinates. Managers constantly wish that employees at lower levels would recognize the common goals of all employees. As authority is delegated to the lowest possible level, subordinates develop this common interest.

Practice Situation

Planning the delivery routes for such a large city was complicated. Jim Bartlett felt he had to draw them up himself because of the importance of speed in the Same-Day Delivery Service he and his wife had started.

Then his delivery drivers began to learn how to make out their own routes. As they learned their territories, he gradually turned over the routing jobs to them.

Although employee routings were not better than Jim's, the drivers began to make their runs more quickly and there were only occasional complaints from customers. Why? The extra authority and the resultant feeling that they were trusted and valued participants in the fledgling company caused the improvement.

Check Points

It may seem contradictory that authority, soundly handled, has the effect of passing this authority out of the hands that exercised it.

The by-products of delegated authority are extremely valuable.

Caution: Sound judgment is required to know what can be successfully delegated and when this authority can be properly handled at a lower level. Delegation must be a gradual process.

Principle IV: Delegated Authority Carries Obligations to Report Back to Those Who Delegate

Authority starts at the top and is passed down to subordinates. The supervisor expects that the subordinate does not go too far afield with the delegated authority, that the subordinate asks questions as to the limits of authority if they are not clear, and that the effects of the authority further down the line are reported back.

Practice Situation

Because of Supervisor Pat Boller's demonstrated competence, he was given authority to handle employee grievances. Yet, as a result, his superior lost his feel for employee attitudes, needed for making policies on other employee matters. He requested Pat to report frequently on the outcome of grievances.

Check Points

Superiors are entitled to adequate communication from subordinates, even though they have delegated authority.

The lack of properly handled authority at a lower level is a major reason that sometimes further authority is not delegated.

A new relationship exists after authority is delegated.

Principle V: Misused Authority Impairs the Success of the Operation

Searching for the individual to blame and discipline, knowing all the answers, making all the decisions, bearing down harder and louder when results fall off, complaining without constructive suggestions to the superior: all of these typical actions tend to impair authority.

Practice Situation
Service to customers had deteriorated badly. Be-

Check Points
Despite pressure from above, Tony Steward

cause his subordinates demanded correction, supervisor Tony Steward could have raised the roof to his employees.

Instead, he described the problem in detail, held skull sessions to get suggestions, and permitted his subordinates to try new approaches. He said 'no' when the ideas were too exotic, but approved some with minor inadequacies.

Improvement came, gradually, but permanently. And the employees started having a good time and generated more enthusiasm for their jobs.

exercised authority in a way that he felt would succeed.

Since authority is earned from below, the privilege may be lost through abuse.

Excessive power plays cause fears. Fears cause subordinates to raise defenses. The emphasis on defense detracts from the fundamental job-centered give-and-take between supervisor and employee.

Principle VI: Improvement in the Skill of Exercising Authority Can be Learned

Improvement in handling the complexities of authority does not automatically occur when an employee is given more and more authority. Improvement does come when experience is based primarily on constant and keen observation of the effects of one's authority on subordinates.

Practice Situation
Supervisor Jo Stokes praised an employee for a job well done. The next time she praised for an adequately done job. The worker began looking to Jo for praise more and more often.

Check Points
The results of authority are all too easily misinterpreted. Jo should find other job-centered goals for the worker, ones that could help her derive her own satisfaction for her

Jo concluded that she should continue praising since the young worker seemed to need it.

work, rather than repeating loose praise.

Supervisors must take the time to look back over actions in order to determine for themselves how their exercise of authority can be improved.

DISCIPLINE

Is discipline a help or a hindrance to effective authority?

The positive discipline becoming prevalent in today's management makes punishment unnecessary.

Discipline is a commonly used action in the exercise of authority. It is obvious that the use of discipline has its limitations, as well as its advantages, in different circumstances.

Let's examine a few of the common misconceptions about discipline and then offer corrections to these ideas.

Misconception: Discipline is an effective way of putting a subordinate in a position in which he or she will not dare to make the same mistake again.

Correction: Discipline can be used as a constructive instructional tool if a detailed explanation is presented of the reason for discipline and of how mistakes can be prevented the next time.

Misconception: When disciplining, an example should be made of the employee since group pressures are supposed to effect improvement.

Correction: Privacy is the sound policy. Since discussion should be corrective, the presence of others is not advised. Also, the presence of an audience risks the possibility of group pressures that work opposite to correction. Humiliation is *never* the purpose of discipline.

Misconception: If an employee does not know any better after several disciplinary actions, discharge is appropriate.

Correction: Before discharging, management has the responsibility to do everything possible to correct the employee in the present job held. If this fails, consideration must be given to qualifications in other work. As a last resort, discharge may be in the best interests of both the company and the inept employee.

SKILL IN EXERCISING AUTHORITY:
SKILL-BUILDING APPLICATION

A leader often wants to know:

1. What has happened to respect for authority?
2. Why is it that people do not treat me well?
3. Why do my subordinates *not* do what I want them to do?
4. Why do people not accept responsibility more readily?

Much confusion exists about the words *authority, exercising authority, responsibility,* and *discipline.* In this chapter, we have examined these questions and terms, and the principles of authority involved.

**Good discipline is the kind of supervision
that makes punishment unnecessary.**

ASSIGNMENT: Six principles of authority were discussed. It is important that you understand these principles. After each stated principle, write in your understanding.

EXERCISING AUTHORITY WORKSHEET

PRINCIPLE OF AUTHORITY   MY UNDERSTANDING

Principle Number 1

Authority is conferred from above but earned from below.

_____
_____
_____
_____
_____
_____

Principle Number 2

The primary goal of authority is job-centered assistance.

_____
_____
_____
_____
_____
_____

Principle Number 3

Important advantages result when authority is passed down the line.

_____
_____
_____
_____
_____

Principle Number 4

Delegated authority carries obligations to report back to those people who delegate.

_____
_____
_____
_____

Principle Number 5

Misused authority impairs the success of the operation.

_____

_____

_____

_____

_____

_____

_____

Principle Number 6

Improvement in the skill of exercising authority can be learned.

_____

_____

_____

_____

_____

_____

_____

IDEAS FOR IMPROVEMENT

From what you have learned in this chapter, list one or more specific actions that you intend to initiate within the next thirty days.

1. _____
   _____
   _____
   _____
   _____
   _____
   _____

2. _____
   _____
   _____
   _____
   _____
   _____

3. _____
   _____
   _____
   _____
   _____
   _____
   _____

REVIEW QUESTIONS

1. T   F   The atmosphere of authority created by the person in the organization above will inevitably affect the atmosphere of authority that a supervisor creates below.

2. T   F   Supervisors cannot nor should they want to insulate themselves from authority from above.

3.   Real authority evolves from _____

    _____.

4. T   F   There is more to authority than the exercise of discipline.

5. T   F   Good team effort rarely occurs without the proper exercise of authority.

6. T   F   It is difficult to obtain respect and confidence of individuals so that they honor authority.

7. T   F   True discipline can never be constructive.

8.   List an example from your own experience in which you feel authority was well handled.

    _____

    _____

    _____

9.   Complete the worksheet in the application section by carefully examining the six major principles of authority and your understanding of each principle.

CHAPTER 12

Skill in Developing People

The more skill a supervisor has in helping employees to grow to their maximum capacity, the more he or she can contribute to the success of the company.

HOW EMPLOYEE DEVELOPMENT PAYS

More than ever, today's supervisor is faced with the need to develop each employee to full potential of his or her abilities, to help each employee make the most of himself or herself, and, in so doing, to build a capable and cooperative work force.

Productive Power

Every company today is looking to its supervisors to increase output, improve service, cut waste, improve methods, and maintain quality—all at lower costs. Employee development is each supervisor's most valuable tool. Its results are tangible, money-saving, and productive.

Changing-Need Skills

Increased mechanization, more automation, and more new developments are occuring more now than ever before in industrial history; and the rate at which these changes and developments are taking place is mind-boggling. To every supervisor, this means that skills must keep in step with the rapid technological advances. You do indeed live in a push-button age, but even more and better-skilled hands are going to be needed to push the buttons.

Employee Relations

Effective development of people has a lot to do with sound employee relations. Here is why: A person who is trained to do a job well has greater job satisfaction because of the feeling that his or her abilities are fully used. This satisfaction in turn reduces absenteeism and turnover, reduces grievances, minimizes accidents, and, above all, improves job interest.

Building Human Resources

Few, if any, companies today have enough human resources for skilled jobs and for promotion up the line. Most companies find that skilled people do not grow on trees. Each supervisor must grow her own.

NOT 'HIT-OR-MISS'

Recognizing that employee training and development pay, how does a supervisor get results that are real? Most supervisors spend a lot of time and effort in improving employee performance. They instruct, they coach, they check. When it comes to getting results, however, they sometimes find themselves falling short of the mark. Too often, they spin their wheels but make no progress.

A skillful developer of people understands and practices this key point: Training must be done in a *planned* and *systematic* way; it cannot be done on a hit-or-miss basis. Just as a supervisor plans schedules, methods, and equipment changes, so must plans be made to develop people.

Planned development includes these two important steps:

1. Find out who is to be trained, what needs to be taught, and what results are expected.
2. Skillfully apply a variety of training methods and tailor them for each employee's needs.

This chapter will discuss ways to spot training needs and also some practical methods for developing people. By mastering the skills mentioned here, you can raise the level of employee performance.

SKILL: Be a Watchful Observer

All of your training problems are right in front of your eyes. You can see them if you develop the habit of carefully observing your employees.

Practice hint: Select a 'best' worker and a 'poor' worker and carefully observe each one at work. By comparing their work habits, job methods, and job knowledge, you will get ideas on how to help your substandard worker improve.

SKILL: Learn to Use Yardsticks

You can make effective use of departmental records as a training tool. Records you can use include records of production, labor turnover, scrap, costs, grievances, absenteeism, accidents. Properly used, these records will point up training problems and will measure your training results.

Practice hint: Follow these two valuable suggestions:

1. At least once a month, review your departmental reports and records. Ask yourself: What is my most critical problem? How did it originate? What training can help solve this problem?
2. To measure your training results, develop a simple control chart. You can plot your group performance on such factors as quality, customer complaints, output, waste, costs, accidents, down-time, turnover, and absenteeism.

SKILL: Inventory Your Employee Capabilities

Supervisors are accustomed to taking inventories of materials, parts and supplies, equipment, and finished products. Why not keep inventories on your most valuable resource—your human resource?

Practice tool: By using a Skill Guide, periodically review *which employees* can perform *what operations* and *how well.*

List employees in left column.

Head vertical columns with different jobs or operations.

Use symbols: (X) excellent skill level

                      (S) satisfactory skill level

                      (O) needs additional training.

At a glance, you will be able to spot training needs and plan the skill development of your employees.

SKILL: Know What is to be Taught

For effective development, a supervisor not only must know who needs training, but also what to teach.

Practice tool: As a guide for on-the-job instruction, use the Job Breakdowns.

SKILL: Plan Your Upgrading

You cannot produce a qualified person for a specific job overnight. The upgrading of skills takes time and planning. As a supervisor, you will want to bring along promotable talent systematically.

Practice pointer: At least once a year, you will find that it pays to list your employees by job classification (name, age, pay, years of service, and years on the job). Then classify them into these three groups:

A. Qualified on present job and can be trained for promotion or transfer.

B. Needs training on present job and may be promotable later.

C. Needs training on present job, but has limited potential for advancement.

You can add categories such as 'Appears to be unqualified for present job,' or 'Will retire in one year and needs replacement trained.'

HOW TO USE TRAINING METHODS

One of your most important responsibilities—and satisfactions— is helping the people you supervise become better people tomorrow than they are today. No one has a better opportunity to do this than you, the supervisor. You are with your workers perhaps eight hours a day, forty hours a week; or more than one-third of their waking life. That is a lot of time to influence someone's development.

These Basic Skills are essential for improving employees' performance on their present jobs; for upgrading employees; and for building a well-informed skilled work force.

Training Skill: How to Job Instruct

Employees are not born with job skills; this is why supervisors must be skilled in teaching the fundamentals of the jobs under their jurisdiction. If employees do not do their jobs properly, chances are it is because they have not been properly instructed.

Method:

1. Get ready to instruct.
2. Prepare the learner.
3. Tell, show, and explain by using a job breakdown.
4. Correct if necessary.
5. Follow up so speed and skill are developed.

When to Use:

1. For teaching skills to new employees.
2. When job methods change.
3. When poor work habits creep in.
4. When a worker is being transferred or promoted.
5. For refresher training.

Training Skill: Reviewing Performance

All of your workers must understand clearly what you expect of them and what you think of their individual performances. For this reason, you must regularly keep track of each person's performance. They cannot possibly be expected to make the changes you want if they do not know what those changes are.

Method:

Using job descriptions or specifications:

1. Review the worker's entire performance.
2. Pinpoint where you think things are going well and state where you desire improvement.
3. Agree on training steps.
4. Train and coach.

When to Use:

1. At least once a year.
2. Before transfers or promotions.
3. To stimulate self-improvement.
4. When an employee is restless about his or her progress.
5. To tune in on employee thinking.

Training Skill: How to Use Job Rotation

Because people learn from experience, job rotation can be profitably used. Job rotation helps the worker develop knowledge, and zest for work. For your department, you build a reservoir of multiskilled employees.

Method:

1. Let workers temporarily exchange jobs. (Be sure you explain why.)
2. Move workers systematically from lower- to higher-skilled jobs. Assign new duties gradually.
3. When feasible, move people from one department to another in a planned way.

When to Use:

1. To prepare for an increase or decrease in work force.
2. To provide back-up workers and to double up on skills.
3. To develop an understudy for various positions.
4. To prepare a worker for promotion.

Training Skill: Develop an Understudy

All stage productions use understudies who learn the lines of the principal characters in order to provide insurance that the show will go on. In the same way, you can build reserve strength in your department.

Method:

1. Spell out the job requirements.
2. Recommend or select the person with highest supervisory potential.
3. Coach by delegating duties.
4. Allow the person to pinch hit for you occasionally.
5. Give the person special assignments.

When to Use:

1. When back-up strength is needed.
2. When you near retirement or expect promotion.
3. To develop a person for another department or to assume part of your duties.

Training Skill: On-the-Job Coaching

More than 80 percent of employee development depends on day-to-day coaching by the supervisor. No employee retains all that has been taught. Moreover, real growth and improvement depend on the personal contact between worker and supervisor and on lots of practice at the newly acquired skills.

Method:

1. Guide each worker on how to improve skills.
2. Recognize good work.
3. Take corrective action on poor work.
4. Build a positive work attitude.

When to Use:

1. Every available hour of each work day.

**Training Skill: Holding
Group Discussions**

Group discussions play an important part in developing employees. They can be used to supplement one-to-one talks in communicating information, to review policies, to get ideas, and to pass along facts about or for the company.

Method:

1. Plan your discussion in advance.
2. Cover only one or two key points.
3. Keep discussion two-way.
4. Try to reach a definite conclusion.
5. Keep discussion to the point.

When to Use:

1. To pass information.
2. To exchange ideas.
3. To help change group attitudes.
4. To build group rapport and pride.
5. To stimulate teamwork.
6. To solve a group problem.

DEVELOPING PEOPLE FOR RESULTS

A successful supervisor gets results by being able to develop people to their highest capacity. A good supervisor understands and skillfully applies the five fundamentals discussed here.

Know Your Workers

When training, remember that no two people are alike. Each person has unique, individual differences in background, ability, experience, and job interest.

Let Learning Take Place by Doing

You can talk to your workers, let them read instructions, have them observe. Skill development, however, begins only when the workers begin doing the job.

Provide Incentive to Learn

For any workers to improve, they must be interested in learning. That is why supervisors must look for ways to inspire employees' desire for self-improvement.

Build on Strengths

A supervisor can develop people more appropriately by knowing what each person's strengths are—what each person can do best. Then, assign jobs and build skills on the basis of these strengths.

Create a Learning Climate

A skillful developer of people knows how to create an atmosphere conducive to learning. You can do this by examining your own attitude toward people, by your real interest in their improvement, and by setting an example through bettering your own performance.

SKILL IN DEVELOPING PEOPLE:
SKILL-BUILDING APPLICATION

The effective supervisor today has developed a skill in helping people grow to their maximum ability. As you have practiced in previous chapters, you must evaluate both your own and your peoples' capabilities. To help you assess and develop people, complete a skills inventory and a job breakdown worksheet.

To develop people, you must match job requirements with the people doing those jobs, and then help them build on their strengths while eliminating some of their job deficiencies.

A skillful developer of people knows that perhaps the most important element of development is to create an atmosphere in which learning can take place. This can happen by projecting the attitude of interest and helpfulness and by demonstrating real interest in growth and development.

JOB BREAKDOWN APPLICATION

ASSIGNMENT: Complete the worksheet that follows. The Job Breakdown exercise is designed to help you more accurately divide the job into its various parts. Do the center column first. The *What* describes the parts of the job. The *How* describes the skills required to do the job. We suggest that you do this exercise to break down a job in your section or department that has several people in the same job classification.

JOB BREAKDOWN	POSITION _____	DEPARTMENT _____
WHEN	WHAT AND HOW	WHY AND PRECAUTIONS

SKILLS INVENTORY APPLICATION

ASSIGNMENT: Use the information from the previous worksheet assignment, specifically the *How*, which implies and describes the skills needed on the job to complete the next worksheet. Across the top of the page, list the skills necessary to do the job function previously described. Next, list the names of all the people in that job classification. Finally, insert the appropriate skill level (X, S, or O) as described on the form.

REMEMBER, RATE THE SKILL LEVEL, NOT THE WORKER'S PERSONALITY.

SKILLS INVENTORY WORKSHEET

JOB SKILLS NECESSARY TO PERFORM JOB

NAME OF EMPLOYEE					

X   Possesses excellent
    skill level

S   Possesses satisfactory
    skill level

O   Needs additional training

In many instances, you, as the supervisor/manager, are concerned not only with present performance, but also with the future performance of the individual. The previous assignments drew attention to *both* the strengths and weaknesses of the individual in relation to his or her current job. This exercise builds on that.

ASSIGNMENT: The names of all persons you supervise (or will be supervising soon) should be included in this exercise. Enter their job classification or title. What is the competency of each person as you see it? The previous exercises may be used to add weight to your opinion.

Competency Level:

A. Qualified and promotable.
B. Needs training. May be promotable.
C. Qualified in present job, but not promotable.
D. Needs training for present job.

PLANNED UPGRADING OF PERSONNEL

Name	Job Classification	Competency Level	Comments

IDEAS FOR IMPROVEMENT

From what you have learned in this chapter, list one or more specific actions that you intend to initiate within the next thirty days.

1. _____
_____
_____
_____
_____
_____

2. _____
_____
_____
_____
_____
_____

3. _____
_____
_____
_____
_____
_____

REVIEW QUESTIONS

1. T F   In order to be successful, training and development of people must be done in a planned, systematic way.

2. T F   If a worker is not performing properly, chances are it is because he or she has not been properly instructed.

3.   More than _____percent of employee development depends on day-to-day coaching by the supervisors.

4. T F   When training, you must consider that no two people are alike.

5. T F   A worker's skill development does not begin until the job is actually started.

6. T F   A supervisor can develop people well if she takes the time to discover what each worker does best and builds on these strengths.

7. T F   A supervisor's attitude toward people is not important.

8.   Identify from your own experience and observation what is the strongest strength within your department.

   _____

   _____

9.   From your experience and observation, list what you feel is the most obvious weakness within the people in your department.

   _____

   _____

10.   Complete the worksheets in the application section, which will inventory you and your fellow workers in your department. Does the inventory reflect the same answers you listed in questions 8 and 9 above?

CHAPTER 13

Skill in Self-Development

T oday's demand for more and better trained people in management places success squarely in the laps of the people who are willing to work for it. Success is not easy to achieve, but at no time in our industrial and business history have there been so many opportunities for competent, qualified people.

SUPERVISORY PROGRESS

Surveys show that the majority of supervisors would choose their present careers if they had it to do over again. Most feel they have made progress. Many feel they would have progressed further in their careers if they had had more formal education.

EDUCATION AND SELF-DEVELOPMENT

Lack of formal education need not hamper the progress of a person if he or she realizes that:

1. Real education is not necessarily formal education. Real education is measured by the openness of the mind and the willingness to study and learn rather than by the number of years spent in school.
2. A college diploma is an added asset at any time and is required in many jobs. Ability, imagination, and energy are equally as important and must be cultivated throughout one's lifetime.
3. It is very important for everyone with or without formal education to read, study, and continue to inform themselves about advances, new techniques, and ideas in their particular field. In our rapidly changing world of technology, it is possible to become obsolete quickly.
4. Today, there are many opportunities for anyone who seeks formal education advancement. There is an even greater wealth of self-development techniques. And, in the final analysis, all development *is* self-development.

FIVE PRACTICAL STEPS TO SELF-DEVELOPMENT

Continued effort at self-development and self-improvement is a conspicuous trait of nearly all people in middle-level and particularly top-level positions.

Self-development may take many forms. It can mean reading a book, attending lectures, joining a club, or taking a course at the local college or university. Not all self-improvement involves technical knowledge. Many companies place an equal or higher value on the ability to get along with people.

You can progress from your present situation to the goal you wish to reach by following five basic steps:

Step I: Defining Your Goal

Although most people will readily admit that they want something more out of life than what they have now, very few will be able to tell you exactly what they expect to be in five years, and then in five years more. Thinking about these expectations may suggest a starting place for your self-development program.

Self-Analysis

Retreat to a quiet place where your thoughts will not be interrupted and begin to make a personal assessment of where you stand right now. Be completely honest with yourself. Ask yourself these questions:

1. Is my personality really acceptable?
2. Do people like me? Respect my opinions?
3. Do I possess all the skills necessary in my work?
4. Do I use my spare time to good advantage?
5. Have I really given my job my best effort?
6. Do I have enough push?
7. What is a leader? Am I one?
8. Do I really like my job, or am I just drifting for lack of ideas or ambition?
9. What are the chances of personal improvement in my present job if I continue on as before?
10. Am I actually inclined toward management development?

By answering these questions, you are stacking yourself up against a success chart you have prepared by yourself, for yourself. By your own self-criticism, you will uncover traits or talents that you individually desire to possess.

Although you may know what talents need brushing up, to get a clearer picture before you establish a fixed goal, talk to someone whose counsel you respect. This person's comments may give you insights into your strengths and weaknesses. Weigh all of these comments as honestly as you can.

Step II: Generate the Drive and Desire

The great hindrance to study is the sense of I have no time. We all have *exactly the same amount of time* available to us as every other person on earth. Everyone has all the time there is, and this excuse means simply that study for advancement is not considered to be as important as some other time-user.

"I just never seem to get time to do that," is a common excuse. An easy test of your interest in anything is to note how much time you find to devote to it.

Some psychologists note that a person's general behavior is guided, both consciously and unconsciously, by a desire to achieve greater happiness. Each person tends to yield willingly to a set pattern of life and will not struggle against the tide unless some dire consequence threatens to disrupt the present course. Thus, an attempt along the lines of self-improvement requires not only a desire to reach a new goal; it also must be coupled with an energetic physical and mental effort.

Step III: Select the Program

Your self-development program may call for formal education, informal study, or a combination of both. Programs most frequently selected by supervisors include those listed below.

Adult Education Courses

Millions of men and women are attending adult education programs offered through public schools and through the vast new network of relatively inexpensive junior colleges that are springing up across the country. Many of these programs are college level courses, but do not necessarily carry with them college credit. Many companies consider these courses so beneficial, however, that they will reimburse employees who successfully complete them.

Home Study Courses

Thousands of people enroll in home study and correspondence courses each year. These courses include private correspondence schools as well as accredited college and university courses and courses offered through educational television programs.

University Extension Courses

These courses may or may not carry college credit. Although they are referred to as *extension courses,* they are often conducted on-campus. They may be taught by regular faculty of the college or university, or by a special department set up by the administration for just such programs. They may also be taught by competent persons in business and industry known to the college or university as being particularly capable in the field concerned.

Company-Sponsored Courses

More and more corporations have some type of 'classroom factory' and regular trainers or instructors who teach in it. In addition, many companies offer avocational programs after hours. These classes are offered to help round out the whole person.

Professional Societies

Many professional societies exist that serve particular industries. These groups sponsor programs that stress their particular interests.

Step IV: Study with a Purpose

Whether you pursue formal or informal programs, there are some things you can do to get the most out of your studies.

Getting the Most Out of a Book

Choosing a Book

1. Consider the author's background and experience to be sure that you will respect, value, and be able to trust what is written.
2. Consider whether the book is written for a person of your education and experience.
3. Be sure that the contents will widen your horizons, that it is not just old hat to you.
4. Choose a book that fits into your self-development needs.
5. If you are not aware of what these books might be, ask your superior or other person whose judgment you trust to help you develop a reading list of books that will be beneficial to your development.

When and Where to Read

1. Shut off the television or radio.
2. Avoid reading where conversation is going on.

3. Try to choose a time when your mind is free from other matters.
4. Try to arrange a long enough reading time to really get into the book.

How to Read

1. Get into the habit of testing yourself at frequent intervals, such as at the end of paragraphs or pages, to be sure you have absorbed what you have read.
2. If you find yourself reading over pages without absorbing, go back and reread.
3. Pause from time to time to think where application of what you are reading may be made to your work or experience.

Read With a Marker in Your Hand

1. If it is your own book, underline passages that impress you.
2. If you come across words you do not understand, look them up in a dictionary and jot the meanings down in the book's margin.
3. Make notations on the flyleaf of page numbers on which ideas of particular interest are to be found.
4. Have a note pad close by on which to jot down things you want to do as the result of ideas suggested by your reading.

Getting the Most Out of a Speech

Where to Sit

1. If you sit in the back of the room, everything that happens in the room distracts your attention.
2. You will be able to hear more distinctly if you sit in front.
3. If the lecturer has charts or exhibits, you will be able to see them clearly.

Taking Notes

1. Writing down special points made by the speaker helps to fix them in your mind.
2. You may make good use of notes if there is an occasion to report the speech to others.
3. Notes will serve as a reminder of what the speaker said. You can use them for future references.

Ask Questions

1. Try to write your questions down while the speaker is speaking. Make your questions short and to the point.
2. Having the question in writing may give you the courage to ask it, whereas if you had to formulate it after you got on your feet, you might hesitate to ask it.

Tell Others

1. Putting the speaker's thoughts in your own words will help to clarify the ideas in your mind.
2. Repeating is an aid to memory.
3. In telling others, you may get reactions that will also be of value to you.

Step V: Measure Your Progress

Living and working do not necessarily result in the improvement of one's education; but continuing to learn while on the job is a bulwark against stagnation and the lowering of job efficiency. It means going forward.

In working your way through this book, you have begun your journey forward. You must continue the giant step you have made in your self-development by taking advantage of every opportunity to continue your growth. Get yourself on the mailing list for seminars and continuing education programs. Make your supervisor aware that you want to take advantage of in-house training and the company reimbursement program, if your company has one. Self-development is on-going; it need never stop. At the end of this book, we have included a list of suggested readings to assist you.

Your supervisor cannot make you a more effective manager. You must do this for yourself. Do not stop with the first hill; climb the mountain.

SELF-ANALYSIS GRID

Although many people like to think in terms of *yes* or *no* absolutes, there are degrees that fall between the *yes* and *no*. This is very true when you analyze yourself. On the Self-Analysis Grid in Figure 10 are some statements against which to judge yourself. Think in terms of "What percent of the time am I. . . ."

STATEMENT	0	10	20	30	40	50	60	70	80	90	100
I am enthusiastic	•	•	•	•	•	•	•	•	•	•	•
I am creative	•	•	•	•	•	•	•	•	•	•	•
I am self-motivated	•	•	•	•	•	•	•	•	•	•	•
I possess self-confidence	•	•	•	•	•	•	•	•	•	•	•
I like my job	•	•	•	•	•	•	•	•	•	•	•
I demonstrate good leadership qualities	•	•	•	•	•	•	•	•	•	•	•
I use my spare time to good advantage	•	•	•	•	•	•	•	•	•	•	•
Others respect my opinion	•	•	•	•	•	•	•	•	•	•	•
I possess all the skills necessary in my work	•	•	•	•	•	•	•	•	•	•	•
I am liked by other people	•	•	•	•	•	•	•	•	•	•	•
I am able to handle criticism	•	•	•	•	•	•	•	•	•	•	•
I accept change	•	•	•	•	•	•	•	•	•	•	•
I am able to connrol my emotions	•	•	•	•	•	•	•	•	•	•	•
I get along with other people	•	•	•	•	•	•	•	•	•	•	•
I get along with my supervisor	•	•	•	•	•	•	•	•	•	•	•
I get along with those I supervise	•	•	•	•	•	•	•	•	•	•	•

Figure 10 Self-Analysis
Grid.

Connect the dots marking your percentage. The area to the left of a line connecting the dots is how you perceive your competence. The area to the right of the line indicates what you perceive as room for improvement.

SKILL IN SELF-DEVELOPMENT: SKILL-BUILDING APPLICATION

Self-development is a continuing process that demands more today than ever before. Industry and business require more and better trained managers and place the responsibility squarely in the laps of the people who are willing to work for it.

You are to be commended for your desire to improve, and for your demonstrated tenacity in getting a job done. If you keep your self-development goals in front of you and continue the same game plan, you will obtain the self-development goals and objectives you will now identify.

ASSIGNMENT: This book has been based on the premise that true development is self-development. The self-development assignment here is to list three well-defined objectives you wish to accomplish within the next year.

MY THREE MOST IMPORTANT OBJECTIVES

Objective Number 1.

What I am doing to accomplish my objective:

_____

_____

_____

_____

_____

Objective Number 2.

What I am doing to accomplish my objective:

_____

_____

_____

_____

_____

Objective Number 3.

What I am doing to accomplish
my objective:

_____

_____

_____

_____

_____

_____

IDEAS FOR IMPROVEMENT

From what you have learned in this chapter, list one or more specific actions that you intend to initiate within the next thirty days.

1. _____

   _____

   _____

   _____

   _____

   _____

   _____

2. _____

   _____

   _____

   _____

   _____

   _____

   _____

3. _____

   _____

   _____

   _____

   _____

   _____

   _____

REVIEW QUESTIONS

1. T F Self-improvement is the planned and continuous process of improving one's knowledge, attitudes and skills, behavior, beliefs, and potential.

2. T F Today's demand for better trained members of management places the responsibility in the laps of those who are willing to work for it.

3. T F A recent survey shows that a majority of supervisors would choose their present careers if they had to do it over.

4. T F Lack of formal education need not hamper your self-development.

5. T F Learning tends to become obsolete rapidly.

6. The five practical steps to self-development are:

   1. _____

   2. _____

   3. _____

   4. _____

   5. _____

7. To define your goal, you need to make an honest personal assessment of where you stand _____.

8. T F Generating the drive and desire is really creating the motivation to want to improve.

9. T F This drive and desire comes from a supervisor who will drive you rather than from within yourself.

10. Complete the self-development assignment in the application section of this chapter by identifying and listing your three most important current objectives.

Answers to Review Questions

**CHAPTER 1: THE SUPERVISOR'S
ROLE**

1. T
2. Profit
3. Service, Product
4. Customer
   Owner
   Community
   Employee
   Itself
5. F
6. Supervision
7. Management
   Employees

8. Material
   Money
   Machinery
   Methods
   People
9. F
10. People

CHAPTER 2: SKILL IN ANALYZING YOUR TIME

1. T
2. T
3. F
4. F
5. must-be-done ring
6. delegation
7. Try to remain calm; Take days one at a time;
   Deal decisively with the problem of the moment;
   Work on the toughest tasks.
8. $625 $62,500
9. You manage time or time manages you
10. (Your answer)

CHAPTER 3: SKILL IN PLANNING

1. a
2. T
3. Planning for training; Planning for cost improvement;
   Planning for changes in processes or quality
   techniques;
   Planning for clerical operations
4. Setting an objective; Forecasting the future;
   Preparing a plan; Including other people
5. T
6. T

7. specific target dates for accomplishment
8. T
9. Letting the demands of the moment outweigh the plans of an entire day; Supervisors who try to go it alone; Maintaining a consistent effort over a long time period.
10. (Your answer)

CHAPTER 4:   SKILL IN DECISION MAKING

1. Your answer
2. T
3. T
4. a company quota goal
5. a company standard of performance
6. Real problem
7. F
8. T
9. T
10. (Your project)

CHAPTER 5:   SKILL IN COMMUNICATION

1. T
2. understanding
3. expressions, gestures, movements, actions, etc.
4. Plan, Explain, Listen, Verify, Evaluate
5. 90 percent
6. F
7. a
8. (Your answer)
9. (Your answer)
10. (Your answer)

CHAPTER 6: SKILL IN TALKING EFFECTIVELY

1. T
2. 10,000–20,000 words
3. F
4. F
5. Refer to pages 75–76
6. T
7. T
8. T
9. (Your answer)
10. (Your answer)

CHAPTER 7: SKILL IN MEMO AND REPORT WRITING

1. T
2. Clearness, Completeness, Candor, Courtesy, Character, Correctness, Conciseness
3. (Your answer)
4. T
5. Self-discipline, Clear thinking, Self-confidence, Job knowledge, Satisfaction

CHAPTER 8: SKILL IN READING FASTER AND BETTER

1. (Your answer)
2. (Your answer)
3. (Your answer)
4. (Your answer)
5. (Your answer)
6. A skill to help pick up the main ideas from reading
7. (Your answer)

8. T
9. T
10. (Your project)

CHAPTER 9: SKILL IN SELLING YOUR IDEAS

1. The capacity to get people to act. The ability to persuade others to support an idea willingly and happily.
2. T
3. T
4. refer to page 115
5. F
6. What will this idea do for me, my department, my company?
7. How or Why
8. T
9. (Your answer)
10. (Your project)

CHAPTER 10: SKILL IN EVALUATING PEOPLE

1. T
2. T
3. F
4. T
5. (Your answer)
6. qualifications
7. (Your answer)
8. (Your answer)
9. (Your answer)
10. (Your project)

CHAPTER 11: SKILL IN EXERCISING AUTHORITY

1. T
2. T
3. competence
4. T
5. T
6. T
7. F
8. (Your answer)
9. (Your answer)

CHAPTER 12: SKILL IN DEVELOPING PEOPLE

1. T
2. T
3. 80 percent
4. T
5. T
6. T
7. F
8. (Your answer)
9. (Your answer)
10. (Your project)

CHAPTER 13: SKILL IN SELF-DEVELOPMENT

1. T
2. T
3. T
4. T
5. T

6. Define goal; Generate desire to get there; Select a program; Study with purpose; Measure your progress
7. now
8. T
9. F
10. (Your answer)

Suggested Reading List

Batten, J.D., *Tough-Minded Management*, American Management Associations, New York, 1969, 1978.

Bittell, L.R., *What Every Supervisor Should Know*, McGraw-Hill, New York, 1974.

Boyd, Bradford, *Management-Minded Supervision*, McGraw-Hill, New York, 1968.

Broadwell, Martin M., *The Supervisor and On-the-Job Training*, Addison-Wesley, Reading, Massachusetts, 1969.

BNA Books, *The Motivation and Measurement of Performance*, Washington, D.C., 1967.

Christen, N.C., *The Art of Persuasion for Sales Managers*, Prentice-Hall, Englewood Cliffs, New Jersey.

Drucker, Peter, *Managing for Results*, Harper and Row, New York, 1964.

Drucker, Peter, *People and Performance / The Best of Peter Drucker on Management*, Harper's College Press, New York, 1977.

Drucker, Peter, *Practice of Management*, McGraw-Hill, New York, 1972.

Drucker, Peter, *The Effective Executive*, Harper and Row, 1967.

Filley, Alan C., and House, Robert J., *Managerial Process and Organizational Behavior*, Scott, Foresman and Company, Glenview, Illinois, 1969.

Gellerman, Saul W., *Motivation and Productivity*, American Management Associations, New York, 1963.

Haldane, Bernard, *Career Satisfaction and Success*, American Management Associations, New York, 1974.

Harragan, Betty Lehan, *Games Mother Never Taught You*, Rawson Associates Publishers, New York, 1977.

Hennig, Margaret, and Jardim, Anne, *The Managerial Woman*, Anchor Press/Doubleday, New York, 1977.

Hughes, Charles, *Goal Setting—Key to Individual and Organizational Effectiveness*, American Management Associations, 1965.

James, Muriel, and Jorgeward, Dorothy, *Winning With People*, Addison-Wesley, Reading, Massachusetts, 1963.

Kanter, Rosabeth Moss, *Men and Women of the Corporation*, Basic Books, Inc., New York, 1977.

Kellog, Marion, *What To Do About Performance*, American Management Associations, New York, 1965.

Koontz, Harold, and O'Donnell, Cyril, *Principles of Management: An Analysis of Managerial Functions*, McGraw-Hill, New York, 1972.

Labor Relations, Plant Engineering, Technical Publishing Company, Barrington, Illinois, 1973.

Leavitt, Harold J., *Managerial Psychology*, The University of Chicago Press, 1972.

MacKenzie, R. Alec, *The Time Trap*, AMACOM, New York, 1972.

Morrisey, George, *Appraisal and Development Through Objectives and Results*, Addison-Wesley, Reading, Massachusetts, 1972.

Nichols, Ralph G., and Stevens, Leonard, *Are You Listening?*, McGraw-Hill, New York, 1957.

Odiorne, George S., *Effectiveness—Direction for Your Success*, DirAction Press, Inc., Minneapolis, Minn. 1967.

Odiorne, George S., *Management by Objectives—A System of Managerial Leadership*, Pitman Publishing Company, New York, 1965.

Oncken, William, and Wass, Donald, *Who's Got the Monkey?*, "Harvard Business Review," November–December, 1974.

Pinkstaff, Wilkinson, *Women at Work, Overcoming the Obstacles*, Addison-Wesley, Reading, Massachusetts, 1979.

Randolph, Robert M., *Planagement*, American Management Associations, New York, 1975.

Schein, Edgar, *Organizational Psychology*, Prentice Hall, Englewood Cliffs, New Jersey, 1972.

Stokes, P.M., *Total Job Training: A Manual for the Working Manager*, American Management Associations, New York, 1966.

Uris, Auren, *Techniques of Leadership*, McGraw-Hill, New York, 1964.

Walters, Roy, *Job Enrichment for Results: Strategies for Successful Implementation*, Addison-Wesley, Reading, Massachusetts, 1975.